Macromedia
Shockwave™
for Director®
User's Guide

Sasha Magee

Noel Rabinowitz

New
Riders

New Riders Publishing, Indianapolis, Indiana

Macromedia
Shockwave™ for Director® User's Guide

By Sasha Magee and Noel Rabinowitz

Published by:
New Riders Publishing
201 West 103rd Street
Indianapolis, IN 46290 USA

Printed in the United States of America 1 2 3 4 5 6 7 8 9 0

Warning and Disclaimer

This book is designed to provide information about the Shockwave plug-in for Macromedia Director. Every effort has been made to make this book as complete and as accurate as possible, but no warranty or fitness is implied.

The information is provided on an "as is" basis. The author(s) and New Riders Publishing shall have neither liability nor responsibility to any person or entity with respect to any loss or damages arising from the information contained in this book or from the use of the disks or programs that may accompany it.

Publisher	Don Fowley
Publishing Manager	David Dwyer
Marketing Manager	Mary Foote
Managing Editor	Carla Hall

Acquisitions Editor
Alicia Buckley

Development Editor
John Kane

Project Editor
Jennifer Eberhardt

Technical Editor
Astrid Javier

Associate Marketing Manager
Tamara Apple

Acquisitions Coordinator
Stacey Beheler

Publisher's Assistant
Karen Opal

Cover Designer
Karen Ruggles

Book Designer
Anne Jones

Production Manager
Kelly Dobbs

Production Team Supervisor
Laurie Casey

Graphics Image Specialists
Clint Lahnen
Laura Robbins
Todd Wente

Production Analysts
Jason Hand
Bobbi Satterfield

Production Team
Heather Butler
Angela Calvert
Kim Cofer
Michael Dietsch
Erika Millen
Scott Tullis
Christine Tyner

Indexer
Chris Cleveland

Dedication

This book is dedicated to our parents:

Pete and Bebe — Sasha Magee
Bobbie and Al — Noel Rabinowitz

Acknowledgments

The authors would like to thank their families for making us who we are (it's their fault!); John, Sarah, Chris, Sheri, Harry, and the rest of the Shockwave team at Macromedia for answering the phone calls and email when we needed help; Astrid Javier for her sharp eye and tongue; David Dwyer, John Kane, Carla Hall, Jennifer Eberhardt and the rest of the New Riders Publishing crew for being crazier than us and doing this book; Jason Rabinowitz for primo (unlicensed) legal consultation; Fred Sharples for the opportunity; Victoria Dawson and Eastman Webber for helping us put food on the table; Rachel Schindler for talking us into doing this; Theo Rodriguez for the fresh beats; Annie Goldsen for the theory and the editing time; Liane Shayer and Laura Cheung for help with the business; Doug Wyrick for the referrals; Heather Rose for making us poster children; Libero Della Piana for strategy and gossip; Amie Fishman, Gretchen Schuessler, Richard Lewis and Chris Daly for picking up the slack; Muddy's for the coffee; Count Basie, Alanis Morisette, The Coup and Public Enemy for the music; Apple Computers, Acclaim Technologies, and Organic Online for their permission to use their movies. Shoutouts to: Scott Kildall, the Director team at Macromedia, Bud, Miles and the Macromedia movers and shakers, Jantje Boichel, Rachel, Ashley, Zachary, Eva, Marvin and Jesse Rabinowitz, Estelle Schneider, Cobie Howard, David Smith, Rob and Sarah and the Oteys, Melvyn, Paulina and Melvyn Jr., Ronetta Walker, Raquel Jones, Richard Taylor, Miguel and Hector, Luis Monterrosa, Sandra and Sonya Loera, Nidal Hussary, Dylan Ryall, Malia and Ronald, Jesse, Nina, Lauren Garlovsky, Josué Guillen, Todd Tollefson, Terrie Albano, David Mertz, Adanjésus Cuávez, Gus, Jarvis, Lee, Judith, Sam, Elena, Joe, Esther, Carol, Bob, Russ, Daisy, Tim, Carolyn, Frank, José, Fred, Tom, Mark, Audrey, Betty, Rich, Ken, Susan, Mavis et al. Cassie and Juan Lopez, Marilyn Bechtel, Arnold Bachetti, Danny, Richard Fallenbaum, Benny Walder, Sharon, Karen, Gerrold, Francisco, Lucy, Edith Laub, Judy Anne Alberti, Claire Burch, Jim Moore, Jane Walford, Bonnie Weiss, Jane Hodes, Aaron Cohen, Mike Napp, Peggy Powell, Miguel Espino, Alfonso, Jon Koritz, Scott Marshall, Rick and Anne and Rachel and Molly Nagin, Danny Queen, Pam Mincey, Francis Calpotura, Mark Toney, Rosie Reyes, Gina Acebo, Danny Rosang, Gary Delgado, Mimi Ho, Loretta Johnson, Jennifer Lynch, Clancy Ward, Laura and Andreas and Paris and Baby X, Ben and Susan Wengrofsky, Jane Heafey, Jung Park, Deborah, Cappy, Steve and Tasha, Mark and Lisa, James Johnson, Kevin and Elizabeth, Shane Zarintash, Norman Ross, Mark Solomon, Roosevelt Washington, May Ying Welsh, Kane Ellen, Wendy, Nady, Kirsten and the HellaVision crew, Roger East, Chuck Duffey, Luann French, Eric Richman, Ed Elkin, Alvin Chau, Media Alliance, Bill Fiore, Therese Bruno, David Howe, Kevin Ellis, Lee Swearingen, Roger Rohrbach, Jeremy Yun, Mel Kangleon, John Dowdell, John Lorance, Rodrigo Flores, Yuval Oren, Peter, Andrew, Bruce and the crew at eline, www.igc.apc.org, Elona Kohn, Sari Gilman, Melani Cammett, Lee Allis, Ed Krimen, Rick Becker, Rocky Mullin, Christine McCarthy, Natalie Zee, Jason Yeaman, Suzanne Lowe, Lina Hoshino, Blake Dawgert, Ray Chen, Abie and Tracy, Eric Hellis, Erich Strom, Dave and Jason (and Mike), Cynthia Miles, Jim Balderston, Rod Amis, Bethany Morgan, Mark Telligan, Homei King, George Williams, Mark Brogger, April Drader, Carl De Cordova, Sean Carney, and to you if by chance your name was omitted in error. You all have shown us good faith and support and we thank you.

Trademark Acknowledgments

Contents at a Glance

Table of Contents

Introduction

Welcome to *Macromedia Shockwave for Director User's Guide*. This user's guide lets you dive right into Shockwave, picking up tips and tricks for making Internet-friendly movies right away. By reading and following along with our step-by-step examples, you will learn to make cool Internet-ready movies in Director.

These Shockwave tutorial movies are made not only to illustrate creative and technical aspects of Shockwave design, but they are also intended to serve as ready-to-use ShockClips, customizable templates, inspirational examples, and thought-provoking brain teasers.

It is the authors' hope that the examples in this book are genuinely useful and not mere abstract exercises. All the tutorial movies here are based on movies designed for the Internet by InfraRed Communications, a leader in Shockwave development and the coauthors' partnership. InfraRed has been doing Shockwave from before the beginning. In June 1995, when Macromedia and Netscape had their Shockwave release party and press conference at Digital World in Los Angeles, InfraRed was there, producing movies that were played live off the Internet—a technological first.

Since then, we—the authors—have been called on to "shock" the Web sites of numerous companies and organizations. Thus, we understand the real-world applications of this technology and the key methods of tailoring Director movies to fit the constraints of Internet delivery. We are not interested in clouding or complicating these methods. If we can shock the Web, so can you.

The tools for creating spectacular multimedia for the Internet are here, and the tools are friendly. The potential is great to use this technology to interact with your market in dynamic and unexpected ways and to express your time-tested messages in this strategic new mass medium. We hope that using this book will demystify the subject and help answer any hesitations or obstacles blocking your effective use of Shockwave.

What This Book Will Do

The *Macromedia Shockwave for Director User's Guide* facilitates your participation in the exciting and explosive field of Internet multimedia. With tools and technologies changing almost daily in this dynamic and somewhat unpredictable new medium, we designed this book to be a lasting resource and reference. The *Macromedia Shockwave for Director User's Guide* details concepts and hands-on techniques you need to use Macromedia's Director for creating true Internet-ready multimedia to be published on the World Wide Web using Shockwave.

The only way to really learn about Shockwave is to do it. So, whether you already think that Shockwave is the best tool for delivering Internet multimedia and want to implement a shocked Web site immediately, or you are just interested in evaluating Shockwave for potential use, it pays to get your hands dirty and experiment.

Who Should Read This Book

This book is for Web designers, multimedia developers, administrators, trend setters, and anyone else who wants to understand and practice the creation of Shockwave movies. Although experienced Director developers may find some of the step-by-step portions of the examples too simple, the Shockwave tips and tricks included here will make the transition to Internet-delivered multimedia as painless as possible.

We assume that the reader has at least some experience working in Macintosh or Windows. Basic familiarity with Director is assumed, although if you haven't used Director much, this is a good way to start learning. We also show techniques that involve Adobe Photoshop, Macromedia SoundEdit 16, Adobe Premiere, Kai's Power Tools, and Fractal Design Painter. For experienced Director users and developers, we have summarized key concepts in sidebars for fast reading.

Note

Although the screen shots in this book show the Macintosh versions of Director and Netscape, the techniques detailed here are equally applicable in Windows, and the menus and commands are identical. We do refer to shortcut keys by their Macintosh names, but in most cases give a Windows equivalent. In the rare cases we do not give a Windows equivalent, because Director is keystroke-compatible between the two platforms, there is an easy translation:

Macintosh Key	Windows Equivalent
Command	Control
Option	Alt
Control	Right mouse button

Example: Command+B in the text becomes Control+B in Windows, and Control+Option+click in the text becomes Alt+right-click.

The final issue here is filenames, which is complicated by the case-sensitive world of Unix, on which HTML is based. Our filename conventions are detailed during the "Spinning Cube Bullets" example in chapter 4.

How This Book Is Organized

Macromedia Shockwave for Director User's Guide is divided into six parts: Prepare to Be Shocked, The Basics of Multimedia on the Internet, Additional Techniques, Lingo Is Your Friend, Exotica, and Appendixes. After you finish each part, you will have a better understanding of how you can use Shockwave to enhance your Web pages.

⚡ **Part One: Prepare to Be Shocked.** Part One gets you up to speed on using the Shockwave plug-in. Chapter 1, "What Is Shockwave?" explores both Shockwave and the limitations of the World Wide Web that led to the development of Shockwave and discusses why you should use Shockwave and how it works. Chapter 2, "Afterburner," examines this file-compression technology built for Shockwave. Chapter 3, "Setting Up Shockwave," shows how to configure your server to recognize and handle Shockwave movies.

⚡ **Part Two: The Basics of Multimedia on the Internet.** Part Two begins the demonstration of creating shocked Web pages. In chapter 4, "Beginning Shockwave Movies," you will learn how to create simple movies, how to use Afterburner to compress those movies, and how to embed the movies in an HTML page. Macromedia uses the term *SiteBytes* to describe small movies that enhance a Web page, and chapter 5, "Introductory SiteBytes," shows you how to create "Hot!" and "New!" siteBytes.

⚡ **Part Three: Additional Techniques.** Part Three takes your Shockwave creativity and productivity to a new level with examples and in-depth discussion of how to shock specific graphics. Chapter 6, "Control Panels and Simple Buttons," and chapter 8, "Diagrams," get right to the step-by-step examples of how to shock these graphics, whereas chapter 7, "Animated Logos," and chapter 9, "Advanced Rollover Buttons," add valuable discussion on these popular graphics.

⚡ **Part Four: Lingo Is Your Friend.** If you hadn't yet realized it, Part Four reaffirms that, yes, Lingo is indeed your friend. Chapter 10, "Basic Shockwave Lingo," uses two examples to illustrate the use of Lingo, Director's scripting language, in working with Shockwave. Chapter 11, "Animating with Lingo," gets you more involved with Lingo, as you both animate an object and follow a cursor with a sprite.

⚡ **Part Five: Exotica.** With the first four parts of the book behind you, you're ready for the advanced applications of Shockwave shown in Part Five. The shocked pages you'll create in chapter 12, "Vertical Movies," demonstrate how using a highly vertical shape can add interest, variety, and utility to a Web page. In chapter 13, "Games," you'll discover another great use for Shockwave as you build the Catch the Blob game. Chapter 14, "Net-Specific Lingo," examines the Internet-specific Lingo that Macromedia has added to Shockwave. And chapter 15, "What Does the Future Hold?" leaves you with some thoughts on the future of Shockwave and the Internet.

⚡ **Part Six: Appendixes.** The book's appendixes give you information on download times for a variety of content sizes and channel speeds, checklists for creating Shockwave movies, a reference on writing HTML for Shockwave, and a reference on new Lingo for Shockwave.

Macromedia Shockwave for Director User's Guide also includes a companion CD-ROM. The CD contains Afterburner for both Macintosh and Windows systems; demo versions of Macromedia's Director and other products used in the making of the book's exercises; all the project files used in the book's examples; final versions of the movies created in this book; and a list of bookmarks to cool Shockwave sites.

Note

To view shocked pages within your Web browser, you need the Shockwave plug-in. This Shockwave plug-in is due to be released after the release date of the Netscape 2.0 Web browser, which had not occurred as this book went to press. A Macintosh version of the Shockwave plug-in was not yet available for inclusion with this book; however, the Windows and Windows 95 pre-release versions of the Shockwave plug-in is included on the CD-ROM.

Note, Tips, Warnings, and Shortcuts

Macromedia Shockwave for Director User's Guide features many special sidebars, which are set apart from the normal text by icons. This book includes four distinct types of sidebars: Notes, Tips, Warnings, and Shortcuts. These passages have been given special treatment so that you can instantly recognize their significance and easily find them for future reference.

Note

A *Note* includes extra information you should find useful. A Note may describe special situations that can arise when you use Shockwave under certain circumstances and may tell you what steps to take when such situations arise. Notes will also provide definitions of terms or topics new to the discussion.

Tip

A *Tip* provides quick instructions for maximizing your productivity when creating shocked pages. A Tip might show you how to speed up a procedure or how to perform one of many time-saving and system-enhancing features.

Warning

A *Warning* tells you when a procedure can be dangerous—that is, when you run the risk of serious problem or error, even losing data or crashing your system. Warnings generally tell you how to avoid such problems or describe the steps you can take to remedy them.

Shortcut

A Shortcut lets you know when you can skip a procedure or set of steps by using a file found on the companion CD-ROM.

Where Do We Go from Here?

Making Shockwave movies is not brain surgery, but it does involve both general and highly specialized types of knowledge. Good use of Shockwave demands technical and creative elegance in your designs. All of your skills and the skills of your team, whether in design, animation, programming, or sound, will be called upon in creating efficient and useful Internet multimedia. It will be well worth your time and effort, and once you roll out your first Shockwave movie onto the Net, you'll never want to stop.

New Riders Publishing

The staff of New Riders Publishing is committed to bringing you the very best in computer reference material. Each New Riders book is the result of months of work by authors and staff who research and refine the information contained within its covers.

As part of this commitment to you, the reader, New Riders invites your input. Please let us know if you enjoy this book, if you have trouble with the information and examples presented, or if you have a suggestion for the next edition.

Please note, though: New Riders staff cannot serve as a technical resource for Shockwave or Director, nor for related questions about software- or hardware-related problems. Please refer to the documentation that accompanies Shockwave or Director, to the Director Help system, or to the Macromedia Web site (http://www.macromedia.com).

If you have a question or comment about any New Riders book, there are several ways to contact New Riders Publishing. We will respond to as many readers as we can. Your name, address, or phone number will never become part of a mailing list or be used for any purpose other than to help us continue to bring you the best books possible. You can write us at the following address:

New Riders Publishing
Attn: Publisher
201 W. 103rd Street
Indianapolis, IN 46290
USA

If you prefer, you can fax New Riders Publishing at 1-317-581-4670.

You can send electronic mail to New Riders at the following Internet address:

ddwyer@newriders.mcp.com

New Riders Publishing is an imprint of Macmillan Computer Publishing. To obtain a catalog or information, or to purchase any Macmillan Computer Publishing book, call 1-800-428-5331.

Thank you for selecting *Macromedia Shockwave for Director User's Guide*!

PART I

Prepare to Be Shocked

CHAPTER 1

What Is Shockwave?

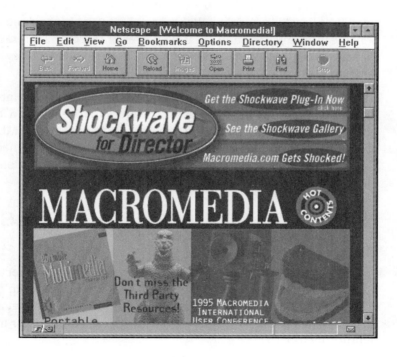

Shock wave n *1: a compressional wave of high amplitude caused by a shock to the medium through which the wave travels. 2: a violent often pulsating disturbance or reaction.*

Shockwave is the marriage of multimedia content to the Internet delivery medium. The key ingredient that Shockwave adds to the World Wide Web is multimedia content created in Director. Director is a powerful and widely used multimedia authoring software made by Macromedia. Director is to multimedia production what PageMaker and QuarkXPress are to desktop publishing: a standard by which all other multimedia authoring environments are measured.

In essence, Shockwave is Director's playback engine plugged into a World Wide Web browser application. Web pages that have embedded Director movies are known as *shocked* Web pages. With the Shockwave plug-in, you can go to shocked Web sites and play their Director movies embedded seamlessly in shocked Web pages. This exciting technical advance enables the engaging and creative power of Director's interactive multimedia to be published on the dynamic, far-reaching, and rapidly expanding Internet.

The advent of Shockwave heralds a qualitative leap in the Internet's power comparable in scope to the invention of the World Wide Web itself. It is not just the addition of a new file type to the HTML standard. Shockwave represents a fundamental shift in the way the medium of the Web will be used and begins to remove some basic limitations previously intrinsic to the Web.

Director and the Limitations of the Web

Since its earliest version in 1985—as VideoWorks 1.0—Director's technology has been a driving force in the multimedia industry explosion. Through continuous innovation and evolution of its tool set and features, Director maintains its position as the world's most popular multimedia authoring tool.

Director is a complete multimedia authoring environment that includes its own easy-to-learn, yet powerful scripting language called Lingo. As you shall see, in multimedia, a little bit of scripting goes a long way in adding interest, interactivity, and variety. Lingo was made to order for the needs of Web scripting.

A strategic strength of Director is its cross-platform compatibility. Director movies move gracefully between the Macintosh and Windows platforms and can be packaged for playback on 3DO and OS/2 as well. By the time you read this book, it undoubtedly will be on several other platforms as well. The capacity for cross-platform playback has been a crucial part of Director's success and also makes Director's technology ideal for the multiplatform landscape of the Internet.

But what exactly does Director do, and why should you use it? Director is an interactive, multimedia, cross-platform authoring tool. Content made with Director is multimedia because it combines text, animation, sound, and video, orchestrating these elements as they play out in time. It is interactive because it can be designed to behave differently based on input from the user via the keyboard, mouse, and so on. Director enables you to provide user control over navigation, ask for responses from your user, and generate feedback based on this interaction.

Navigation control, user response, and feedback all help to make Director an interactive multimedia tool. These characteristics also are hallmarks of the World Wide Web.

Navigation control, user response, and feedback all help to make Director an interactive multimedia tool. Shockwave brings these benefits to the World Wide Web. But doesn't the Web do this without Shockwave? Strictly speaking, the World Wide Web already is an interactive multi-media environment. Yes, Web pages can contain text and bitmapped graphics together, but sound and video files are downloaded and played back separately within helper applications. And yes, hot spots, menus, and query fields all provide interactivity, but this type of interactivity cannot be compared to the instantaneous feedback of even the simplest kiosk or computer game! Fast feedback, present in Director movies but absent in the unshocked Web, draws users in, giving them the almost tactile sensation of affecting their environment. And, of course, Shockwave adds animation and sound to the Web.

Without integral sound, motion, and tactile interaction, the communica-tion potential of the Web has been seriously hampered. Before Shockwave, multimedia on the Web was more like multipersonality disorder. Text and bitmaps were integral on the page, but sound and video lived isolated in their lonely windows, unsynchronized, disintegrated, and out of context. Animated or sync-sound messages could be offered only via QuickTime or Java. Large QuickTime downloads are slow and nonresponsive at best, and at worst are not an option at all for most users. Java applets are very costly to author, and Java's implementation of multimedia is limited.

Shockwave bursts through these barriers by utilizing Director's power to drastically shrink both the development costs and the network bandwidth needed to convey sound and motion on the Internet. QuickTime and MPEG movies basically work by blasting a series of bitmaps onto the screen. While this can have excellent results, it results in huge files and glacial downloads. Director handles general animation in a more compact and efficient way—sprite-based animation.

A *sprite* is a bitmap that is given a position on the screen at a particular moment in time. A series of sprites can be shown in rapid succession, thus creating animation. In Director, multiple sprites based on the same bitmap can be displayed at once. Sprites can also be stretched, blended, or given color effects. Text can be rendered to the screen in real time with whatever sizes, fonts, and color effects you assign. You can also add QuickDraw (vector-based) objects such as lines, circles, and rectangles. This gives you a wide range of tools to animate images using very little file size to do so.

Director is a time-tested and comprehensive authoring tool. It has been used for many years to author games, marketing tools, CD-ROM titles of every kind, corporate presentations, speaker support, simulations, prototype interfaces, movie storyboarding, and much more. Now with Shockwave, you can leverage much of this mountain of content—with a little elbow grease—for publication on the Internet.

Why Should You Use Shockwave?

Why use Shockwave? When a wave hits, you can either ride it or go under. You'll want to ride the Shockwave wave for the following reasons:

- ⚡ Shockwave is widespread, able to reach a massive audience; it is, therefore, a strategic mass medium in its own right.

⚡ Shockwave adds to existing Web technology by being HTML-compliant. This feature makes it easy to update your current Web pages for Shockwave.

⚡ Shockwave uses the Director engine for the best Internet multimedia with the least-expensive and fastest development.

⚡ Shockwave adds rich media to your Web pages without big bandwidth.

⚡ By adding animation and sound to your Web pages, Shockwave enables many new uses for the Web.

⚡ As more and more sites begin to use Shockwave, sites that don't will be left behind.

The World Widespread Web

All the most popular Web browsers will incorporate the Shockwave plug-in. At press time the Shockwave plug-in has been implemented or announced for Netscape, SGI's WebFORCE, The Microsoft Internet Explorer, and CompuServe. This represents 80 percent of all users of the Web, or an estimated 15 million users.

Utilizing Current Web Technology

Director movies with their DIR file extension are recognized in the HTML standard. DIR files have their own MIME type. There is a new HTML tag, **<embed>**, which references the URL of your Director movie and positions the playback stage within your Web page.

Incorporating DIR files into your HTML is just as easy as embedding a GIF or any bitmap. In fact, much of the work to be done in shocking the Web is immediate replacement of static bitmaps with animated versions of your familiar billboards and logos. In terms of updating your HTML, it couldn't be easier. To include a GIF image in a Web page, for example, you could use the following line:

```
<img src="fish.gif" height=48 width=64 alt="Fish image">
```

The process of embedding a Director movie is just as simple:

```
<embed src="fish.dcr" height=48 width=64 alt="Fish image">
```

Director Is the Standard

There are more than 250,000 multimedia developers already using Director. Director was designed to be approachable as well as powerful, and is being used in many diverse settings including in-house corporate communications departments, interactive titles development, game development, and more. It has proven to be the most enabling technology for multimedia in general.

In contrast, Sun Microsystems' Java development language is significantly more complex. While Java is a tremendous advance for the Internet, it is not the best choice for multimedia. Because Java is a full-blown programming language, it has a much higher learning curve. Just as not everybody can learn to use C++, not everyone can afford the commitment to learn Java. Every example in this book would take many times as long to develop in Java as it did in Director, even after you had learned the language.

The second advantage Director has over Java for multimedia is its robust multimedia feature set. In Director's 10 years of evolution, Macromedia has included a large number of built-in multimedia features that make development of animations or interactive multimedia pieces downright easy, and often even fun. Director takes care of the dirty work, handling things like layering, interpolated motion and timing, leaving you free to actually communicate.

Rich Media, Thrifty Bandwidth

Shockwave is perfect for adding rich media to your Web pages. By using sound and animation, shocked Web sites command more attention, have more impact, and are more memorable.

Every Web user has had the experience of waiting for a graphic-laden page to download. With the advent of motion-based media such as QuickTime, this problem only gets worse. Shockwave, however, makes very efficient use of bandwidth, often better than static images.

It's not just what you say, it's how you say it. Why is integrated multi-media so much cooler than scattered partial-media? TV-like experience, sound, helpful eye-grabbers to guide the user, better user feedback, and complex behavior.

New Capabilities Means New Applications

With the new capabilities Shockwave adds to the Web, new applications become possible. Things like real-time graphing, games, and puzzles are things you can create with Shockwave today. Shockwave developers have only scratched the surface of the new possibilities, however, and the near future will bring many new uses as yet undreamed-of.

Shockwave Is Becoming the Standard

As more and more sites are shocked or Java-enhanced, users will come to expect motion and rich interactivity. Sites which use only static graphics will seem like all-text sites do today—old-fashioned.

How Does Shockwave Work?

The plug-in architecture that is being developed for Netscape Navigator, SGI's WebFORCE, and other browsers allows new features to be added to HTML. When the Shockwave plug-in is installed, most of the more popular browsers will recognize the `<embed>` tag, and from what the server tells them is embedded, will be able to pass that information along to the plug-in.

Note

The process by which HTTP (HyperText Transfer Protocol—what the Web is based on) deals with different file types is this:

The server has a MIME-type table that tells it that files of a given extension are a certain type of file. Files with a GIF extension are type image/gif, for example; files with a JPG extension are image/jpeg; and files with a DCR or DIR extension are application/x-director. Chapter 3, "Setting Up Shockwave," outlines the process of setting up your server in more detail.

Plug-in architecture enables playback of Director movies embedded in your Web pages. Easy as pie. With a Shockwave-compatible browser, DIR and DCR files become just another file type, like GIF or JPEG. Just like embedded GIFs or JPEGs, your Shockwave movie files download with the Web page, then the Shockwave plug-in plays your movie in the page.

Shockwave inherits nearly all of the tremendous multimedia power of Director. With the exception of linked media and XObjects, your only constraint is download time. For fast downloads, you need small file sizes. Because Director dates from the days of single-sided disks, it is a natural for a world of 14.4 and 28.8 Kbps modems. With the addition of Afterburner, Director's built-in thriftiness with disk space becomes downright miserly. Director's stinginess with disk space, though, doesn't come at the price of power. The examples in this book demonstrate the power that Shockwave can pack into a tiny file.

 Note

The major limitations of Shockwave—no linked media and no XObjects—are no accident. Macromedia had good reasons for not putting either one in Shockwave.

With linked media, it is possible for a movie to have downloaded without the associated files. This would obviously cause problems.

XObjects, by definition, do things that Director does not. These things, unfortunately, can include nasty stuff like formatting your hard drive or trashing crucial files. Since currently there is no way to ensure that any XObject you download is safe, Macromedia has disabled that feature altogether. The folks at Macromedia are looking for a solution, however, and a later version of Shockwave will probably have XObject support.

This chapter should have given you an idea of what Shockwave is and why you should use it. In the next chapter, you explore an unassuming application that gives Shockwave much of its power—Afterburner.

CHAPTER 2

Afterburner

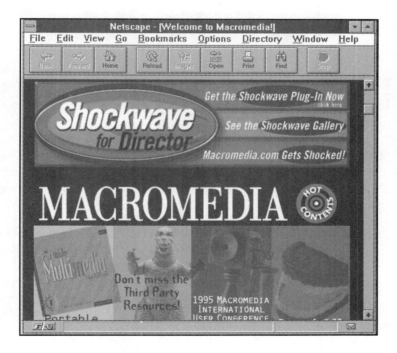

U sually when people think multimedia, they think CD-ROMs and huge file sizes, so the notion of publishing multimedia on the Internet may seem a bit absurd. As we have shown, however, we can use Director to provide media-rich content with file sizes that are consistent with current Web-page norms. Delivering great content under 100 KB is no problem.

Director's architecture behaves like a compression scheme, but it works in the opposite way as QuickTime or Video for Windows. QuickTime and Video for Windows take a series of frames and a continuous soundtrack and work backwards, removing visually redundant information within or between these frames to reduce file size. Director works the other way. It starts compactly, and taking your cast of small bitmap images and sounds, Director expresses or composes them as sprites on the screen in real time to create animated motion. There is no need to remove redundant information from between the frames; that's inherent in how Director works.

Note

> *Compression* is a term applied to all methods of reducing file sizes or bitstreams. Every form of compression has a CODEC (COmpressor/ DECompressor) algorithm, which enables computers to shrink or compress file sizes and then expand or decompress the file later.

Director can also render TrueType and PostScript text, as well as QuickDraw objects such as lines, circles, and rectangles, to the screen in real time. This enables you to build complex motion and imagery without creating a huge file. But the compression doesn't stop there.

Compressing digital files has the benefit of reducing the bandwidth needed to store or transmit that file. For our purposes, compression means faster downloads and richer media in Shockwave. Understanding that download time and thus file size is of paramount importance in Internet multimedia, Macromedia built a dedicated file compression technology for Shockwave called Afterburner.

Working with Afterburner

Afterburner takes in Director movies (DIR files), crunches them down in size, and spits them out as DCR files (for Director CompRessed). These

DCR files are zapped across the Net, then decompressed and played back by the Shockwave plug-in. The process is often referred to as *burning* a file, and the resulting compressed files are often called *burnt files.*

In Shockwave, Afterburned files play back just like the uncompressed original Director file. There is no loss of performance. The only thing you lose is another excuse to take a coffee break while waiting to download uncompressed files.

Note

The first release of Afterburner simply compresses graphics files. Future releases, however, will include audio compression and more graphics compression options.

The main use of Afterburner is to easily and quickly reduce the download time of your shocked Web pages. Afterburner can reduce download times by 40–70 percent. Conversely, Afterburner enables you to include much more content within a file the same size as an unburnt movie.

Afterburner opens up a whole world of creative possibilities to Web designers because it effectively gives you approximately twice the bandwidth to play in. This will enable much more detailed images, more sound, and more involved interactivity.

Note

Interestingly, Afterburner has proven in many cases to be a more compact technique for compressing static bitmaps than GIF or JPEG. One test, for example, discovered that a Director movie that contains just an 8-bit PICT image of 132 KB can be turned into a 44 KB DCR. Imagine that! The same image saved as a GIF is 77 KB!

As Shockwave is becoming a standard for the well-equipped Web user, it makes sense to use Afterburned movies not only for animations and sound, but for simple static images as well. Of course, compression will vary case by case, but in general, the compression ratios in Afterburner are phenomenal.

How Good Is Compression with Afterburner?

In evaluating the usefulness of any compression scheme, you have to ask several questions. What is the compression ratio? Is it lossless or lossy? What are the processing requirements for both compression and decompression? The following sections answer these questions.

Compression Ratio

Comparing the size of the uncompressed Director file with the compressed Afterburner file yields what is known as the compression ratio for Afterburner. There are several factors that determine how small a Director movie will burn. For one thing, Afterburner does not yet compress the audio portion of the DIR file (the sound cast members). It is a real winner, however, in compressing the bitmapped cast members.

Compression Schemes: Lossy and Lossless

In general, compression schemes are either lossless or lossy (no better words have been invented, unfortunately). *Lossy compression* shrinks file sizes by permanently removing nonessential, irrelevant, or redundant information. The resulting file is forever degraded. This is an acceptable compromise for many kinds of media files for which quality is happily sacrificed for a commensurate reduction in file size. There are many sophisticated lossy compression schemes, such as MPEG, JPEG, and Cinepak, but we are not so concerned with them here.

The most direct method of lossy compression is to simply throw out information, a technique called *bit reduction*. Reducing the bit depth or the resolution of bitmapped images, for example, dramatically reduces file size, as does reducing the sampling frequency or bit depth of audio files. For images, dithering can be used to lessen the degradation that results, and lost color information can be restored or simulated later using other techniques. We use these methods frequently when authoring Shockwave movies.

Lossless compression reduces file sizes without degradation or change to the file. PKZIP and StuffIt are examples of tools used for lossless compression (in fact, they use a very similar algorithm to Afterburner's). Lossless compression is extremely important for compressing data that cannot lose even one bit of information, or it becomes useless. Director files made for Shockwave contain precise information for animation, as well as Lingo code for interactivity and so on, so lossy compression schemes cannot be used on Director movies.

Note

The process that PKZIP, StuffIt, and Afterburner use to compress a file is too complicated to go into in any detail here, but a quick summary will give you an idea of what compression ratios to expect.

The compressor looks for repeated patterns of data and keeps what is essentially a glossary of each of those patterns. It then replaces each pattern with the index reference, which is, in general, much smaller. In addition to the compression of Afterburner, Director itself deals with a string of repeated values (such as in a solid-color portion of an image). An uncompressed series of four red pixels in an 8-bit image would require four 8-bit bytes of data, because it would be represented as *red, red, red, red.* Compressed, however, that same series of pixels would take only two bytes of data, because it would be represented as *four red.* This compression process is called *run-length encoding.* As you work with Shockwave, you will discover that images with large areas of solid colors compress very well.

Afterburner takes Director movies (DIR files), applies lossless compression to them, and saves them as Director CompRessed movies (DCR). The reason DIR and DCR files play back identically in Shockwave is that once decompressed, the DCR file is identical to the original DIR file.

In this chapter, you have learned the power of Afterburner, which offers 40–70 percent ratios of lossless compression. It has become an essential enabling technology of Internet multimedia. In the next chapter you learn what is involved in setting up your Web server and browser so that you can use Shockwave.

CHAPTER 3

Setting Up Shockwave

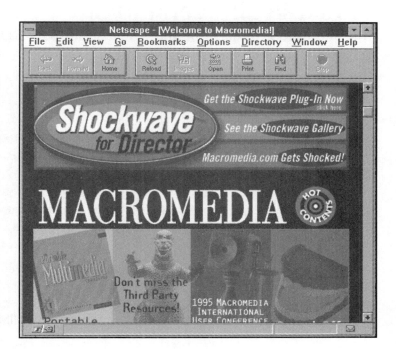

B efore you dive in to Shockwave, you first need to be familiar with some basic World Wide Web terminology. You also need to set up your system. This setup has two steps: setting up your client machine and setting up your server. You can follow the steps in this book without a configured server by simply opening the files from your hard disk. To actually serve Shockwave movies, however, you need to configure your server as well.

Warning

Because Shockwave is a new technology, the steps detailed here may change. We suggest you confirm the exact steps for your system by checking the Macromedia Shockwave site at **http://www.macromedia.com/Tools/ Shockwave**.

Basic Web Terminology

The URL, uniform resource locator, is the standard address for anything on the Internet. A URL has three parts.

⚡ The first part is the name of the Internet protocol. Examples of this include FTP, gopher, HTTP.

⚡ The second part is the name of the Internet host. Examples of hosts include `www.macromedia.com` or `ftp.macromedia.com`.

⚡ Lastly, the address includes the folders your browser has to go through to find the file you're searching.

Our shocked home page, for example, is located at `http://www.eline.com/ Infrared/Shocked`. In this URL, the name of the protocol is `HTTP`, the server is `www.eline.com`, and the path to the file is `/Infrared/Shocked`.

An HTTP server is a computer that delivers World Wide Web data across the Internet. HTTP stands for "HyperText Transport Protocol." In response to a request specifying a URL, the HTTP server returns a block of data, plus the type of that data. The data type is called a MIME type.

A MIME type is a specification of the type of a block of data. MIME stands for "Multi-purpose Internet Mail Extensions." It was originally proposed and used for enriching the content of mail messages. In the context of the World Wide Web, and HTTP in particular, MIME types specify what type of data is returned from a server. MIME types can include text, graphics of various types (GIF, JPEG, PNG, and so on), sound, or Director movies. A MIME type consists of two parts, the content type and the content subtype. The content type specifies a major category, such as image, audio, or application. The subtype specifies a particular data type within that category, such as MIME type of image/jpeg. In the case of a Director movie, the MIME type is "application/x-director".

Configuring the Client

Following are instructions for installing the Shockwave plug-in under Netscape for Windows. If you are using a different browser supported by Shockwave or are on a different platform, check the Macromedia Web site for more information.

1. Locate your Netscape directory and then locate the Shockwave package "sw1b2a32.exe". Double-click it. This will extract the compressed files in a DOS window. Close the window when it's finished.

2. Locate your Netscape directory and double-click the file called "setup." There are two files named "setup," so make sure that you choose the one with the little computer icon next to it.

3. Once the installer has launched, read the instructions on the Setup for Shockwave License Agreement. Choose NEXT if you accept the terms of the agreement. If not, choose EXIT. On the second screen, under destination directory, choose NEXT. Shockwave for Director will be installed.

4. This will install the Shockwave Plug-In into the default directory, which is listed uder "Destination Directory."

5. If there is no text under the "Destination Directory," choose BROWSE, and select the directory where Netscape resides. Then choose NEXT to continue installing.

6. Read the "readme.txt" information. If, after completing this process, you get error messages from Netscape while viewing a "shocked" Web page, try re-extracting the Shockwave Package you downloaded, and follow the "Extracting" instructions again.

Configuring Your Server

To successfully serve Shockwave movies, your HTTP server must be configured to recognize and handle Shockwave movies. Most servers are Unix-based platforms, although some servers use Macintosh HTTP or WebSTAR software. This section covers configuration for Unix, MacHTTP, and WebSTAR servers.

Configuring Unix Servers

Have your system administrator create an entry in the file that registers MIME types. The administrator will need the following information:

> MIME type: application
>
> Sub Type: x-director
>
> Extensions: DCR, DIR, DXR

Configuring Macintosh Servers

Macintosh Web servers come in two flavors: MacHTTP, which is shareware, and WebStar, which is a commercial product. Although WebStar is based on MacHTTP, they have different configuration processes.

Configuring MacHTTP Servers

If you are running a MacHTTP-based HTTP server, you need to modify the file MacHTTP.config. Add the following lines to the file:

> BINARY .DIR TEXT * application/x-director
>
> BINARY .DXR TEXT * application/x-director
>
> BINARY .DCR TEXT * application/x-director

Configuring WebSTAR Servers

If you are using WebSTAR, perform the following configuration steps:

1. Run the application WebSTAR Admin.

2. Locate and select your server in the Pick A Server window (your server must be running).

3. Choose Suffix Mapping from the Configure menu. The Suffix Mapping dialog box appears.

4. Specify the following settings:

   Action: BINARY
   File Suffix: .DCR
   File Type: TEXT
   Creator: *
   MIME Type: application/x-director

If you are providing DIR or DXR movies, repeat the process for each suffix you want to add.

Now that you have successfully configured your client and server platforms, it is time to get started with Shockwave.

PART II

The Basics of Multimedia on the Internet

CHAPTER 4

Beginning Shockwave Movies

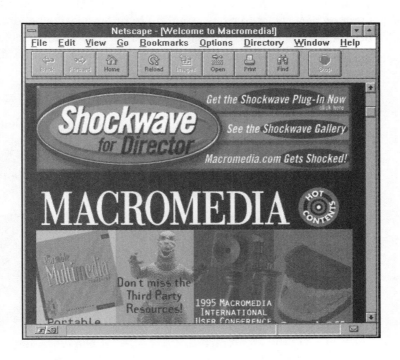

This chapter introduces you to the basics of creating Shockwave movies. You learn how to create the simplest of movies, how to use Afterburner to compress those movies, and how to embed the movies in an HTML page.

This chapter uses bullets as examples of basic multimedia found on Web sites. After you work through the exercises in this chapter, not only will you see how you can create shocked Web pages, you also will have some spinning and flashing bullets you can use on your own Web pages.

EXAMPLE 4-1:

Spinning Cube Bullets

In this example, you learn how to make a decorative movie that can function as a bullet to draw attention to or emphasize headings. You bring the actual bullet into Director and set it as a movie, compress the movie in Afterburner, and finally embed the movie in an HTML page.

Creating the Director Movie

First, you need to bring the cube into Director and set it spinning.

1. Open Director.

2. Choose File, Movie Info. Set the Default Palette pop-up to System Windows and choose OK.

Note

Because the Macintosh and SGI handle Windows palettes better than Windows handles Mac palettes, you will want to create the movie with a Windows palette. Setting the Default Palette to System Windows ensures that all imported files will be dithered to the correct palette.

3. Choose File, Import to display the Import File dialog box.

4. On the *Macromedia Shockwave for Director User's Guide* CD-ROM, find the Ch04/Pix folder, then press Open and select Import All. The eight images of the cube will appear in the Cast window.

5. Choose File, Preferences to display the Preferences dialog box, and set the stage size to 32×32. Set the Stage Location, Top to 22, Left 16. Click OK.

Warning

If you do not set the stage location, Top to more than 20, on the Macintosh the stage will disappear under the menu bar. This makes it very difficult to work on.

6. Select the eight cube files in the cast and choose Cast, Transform Bitmap. Set the Scale value to 50 percent. Click OK.

7. Select the eight cube images in the cast window and Option-drag (Alt-drag in Windows) them to channel 1, frame 1 of the score. Holding down the Option (Alt) key distributes the cast members across time so that they appear sequentially (see fig. 4.1).

8. Use the arrow keys to position the cubes on the stage so that the actual cube images are centered.

Figure 4.1
The cube cast members laid out in the score.

9. In frame 8 of the score, select the script channel and click on the script bar at the top of the score window. The script window appears.

10. In the script window, type the following script:

```
on exitFrame
  go frame 1
end exitFrame
```

The movie is now essentially complete (see fig. 4.2). Save it as spincube.dir. You can run it by pressing Command+P (Control+P in Windows).

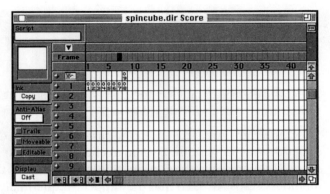

Figure 4.2
The final score layout of the Spinning Cube movie.

Warning

Although movies will loop by default when played in Director, they will not when they are played in Shockwave. Therefore, you must explicitly loop them with a script as shown in step 8. Even movies that do not loop should have the following script in the last frame:

```
on exitFrame
  go the frame
end exitFrame
```

If the movie simply ends, Shockwave will not update the movie's stage area, so dialog boxes or other objects that cover the stage will make it look messy, at best. One way to ensure that you remember to loop the movies is to turn off looping in Director. This can be done by choosing Edit, Loop or by clicking on the loop button on the control panel (the second button from the right).

Compressing the Movie

Now you compress the movie for shorter download times.

1. Drag the spincube.dir movie file onto the Afterburner application. Or, open Afterburner and choose File, Open to open the file.

2. A typical save dialog box with a default name of spincube.dcr appears. Choose the folder Chapters/Ch4/Movies to save the file in and choose OK.

Embedding the Movie in an HTML Page

You now are ready to embed the movie in an HTML page. Because the movie is intended as a bullet, you embed it inline with a line of text.

1. In your Web browser application, open the file ex4_1.htm in the Chapters/Ch4/ folder.

   Note the bullet chart, with boring, static graphics. Close the file.

2. Open the ex4_1.htm file in a text-editing application.

3. Everywhere you see the tag `<img src="Images/bullet.gif" align=left height=16 width=16>` change it to `<embed src="Movies/spincube.dcr" align=left height=16 width=16>`.

4. In your Web browser, open the file again. You should now see the spinning cube bullets (see fig. 4.3).

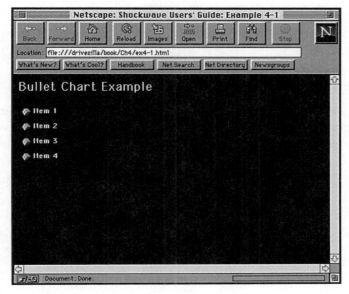

Figure 4.3
The ex4_1.htm file with spinning cube bullets.

Note

> **Filename and Directory Conventions**
>
> There are as many ways to set up a Web site as there are people setting them up. Because the conventions are somewhat arbitrary, for the purpose of this book we will use the same conventions used on our Web site. Please feel free to modify them for use on your site.
>
> We follow three basic rules:
>
> - Filenames are all lowercase and adhere to DOS limitations (8.3 character limit, all alphanumeric characters plus _ and -).
>
> - Directory names all start with a capital letter, for example, Movies or Shockwave.
>
> - Any movies embedded in a page are located in a Movies subdirectory of the directory in which the page exists. Images embedded in a page are located in an Images subdirectory. We make exceptions for images or movies that are used repeatedly on pages in different directories, but this is the general rule.
>
> If you use these examples on a Macintosh or run them from a Unix server, the case of the filenames is important. If, however, you use them strictly on a PC, the case of the file and directory names will not matter.

In the next example, you create a different kind of bullet to use as an attention-getter for additions to your Web site.

EXAMPLE 4-2:

Tiny New Bullet

This is a very small Director movie suitable for marking inline things that may be new to your Web site. Many other concepts are candidates for similar treatment, such as "Improved," "Cool," or "Hot!". In chapter 5, you create a bigger New! movie that will really draw attention to new things on your site.

Creating the Director Movie

This movie is even simpler to create than the preceding one.

1. Open Director.

2. Choose File, Movie Info. Set the Default Palette pop-up to System Windows and choose OK.

3. Choose File, Preferences and set the stage size to a width of 32 and a height of 12. Set the vertical location of the stage to Top 22.

4. Choose Window, Paint to open the paint window.

5. Select the Text tool.

6. Click on the paint window.

7. Using the Font, Style, and Size commands within the Text menu, specify Helvetica, bold, and 10 point.

8. Type `NEW!`.

9. Close the paint window.

10. Drag the cast member from the cast into frame 1, channel 1 of the score.

11. Make the score window the frontmost window.

12. In the Ink pop-up menu, select Background Transparent.

13. Open the control panel (choose Window, Control Panel).

14. Click on the stage color chip to display the background color pop-up and select red. This sets the stage color to red.

Warning

Stage color is a useful way to add variety to your movies. A large number of movies all in a white rectangle gets boring pretty quickly. Stage color is also a useful way to make your movies blend into the window background.

Because people can have some pretty perverse window colors, we suggest you explicitly set the background color of your HTML pages with the `<BODY BGCOLOR=#??????>` tag. The example files on the CD all use this tag. The numbers after the pound sign are hexadecimal expressions of the red, green, and blue values.

15. In the score window, Option-drag (Alt-drag in Windows) the sprite in frame 1, channel 1 to frame 2, channel 1. This makes a copy of the sprite in frame 2.

16. In the Ink pop-up menu, select Reverse.

17. In the script channel of frame 2, click on the script bar and type the following script:

```
on exitFrame
  go frame 1
end exitFrame
```

18. Run the movie. The word *New!* should flash white and black (see fig. 4.4).

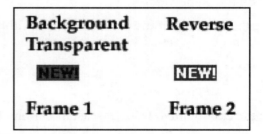

Figure 4.4
The two frames of the finished tinynew.dir movie.

19. Save the movie as tinynew.dir.

Compressing and Embedding the Movie

1. Drag the file onto Afterburner. A save dialog box with a default name of tinynew.dcr appears. Choose the folder Chapters/Ch4/Movies in which to save the file and choose OK.

2. Open the file ex4_2.htm in the Chapters/Ch4/ directory and change the `<em>NEW!</em>` tag in one of the lines of the list to
   ```
   <embed src="Movies/tinynew.dir" height=16 width=32
   alt="NEW!">.
   ```

You are now ready to admire your handiwork. Open the ex4_2.htm file in your browser. Note how your attention is drawn to the line with the movie on it.

In this chapter, you learned to create (very) basic Shockwave movies and how to use the embed command to place the movies on an HTML page. In the next chapter, you create some more basic movies, but in the process you begin to expand your toolkit with some Shockwave essentials.

CHAPTER 5

Introductory SiteBytes

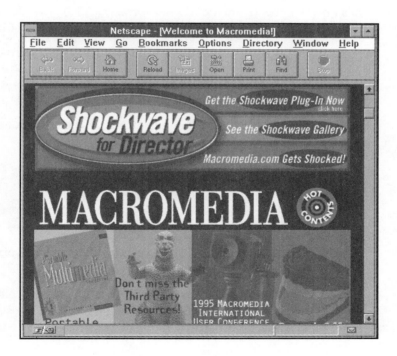

SiteBytes is the name that Macromedia has given to small movies that enhance a Web page. SiteBytes often replicate the function of many of the most common graphics on the Web, such as New!, Under Construction, and so on. In this chapter you create two examples of SiteBytes and, in the process, learn a number of basic techniques for creating effective Shockwave movies.

<u>EXAMPLE **5-1**:</u>

Hot!

This is another attention-getter, like the Tiny New Bullet example from chapter 4. It shows how cycling graphics can make an effective eye catcher. The procedure for making the graphics requires Photoshop and Kai's Power Tools (from MetaTools, formerly HSC). The files are also available on the *Macromedia Shockwave for Director User's Guide* CD-ROM.

Preparation: Copy the Ch05 folder from the CD to your hard drive.

Creating the Flaming Letters

First, you need to create the flaming letters. This can be done in Photoshop 3.0.

Shortcut

If you do not have Photoshop 3.0, Kai's Power Tools, or just want to get straight to Director, you can use the example files hot1–4.pic and fire.pic from the Ch05/Src folder of the CD-ROM.

1. Open Photoshop. Create a new file, sized 64×20 pixels, with a white background.

2. Click on the image with the text tool. Choose a font with a heavy weight (we used Helvetica Black). Set the size to 24 and the spacing to –1.

3. Type **HOT** in the text box and choose OK.

4. Position the text so that it is centered in the image.

5. Choose Select, Save Selection and accept the default parameters.

6. Choose Filter, KPT, Texture Explorer. (The figure is from version 2.0.)

7. In Texture Explorer 2.0, select Fire, Fiery Plasthma from the Presets menu and choose OK (see fig. 5.1). In version 3.0, select the Hot Codons texture from the Presets menu and manipulate it until it looks like fire. Click OK.

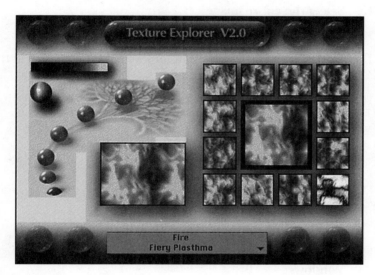

Figure 5.1
Select Fiery Plasthma from the Presets menu.

8. Choose File, Save a Copy. Choose PICT from the Type pop-up menu and name the file hot1.pic.

9. Choose Filter, KPT, Texture Explorer again.

10. Click on one of the tiles that looks similar to the one in the middle. Choose OK.

11. Choose File, Save a Copy. Choose PICT from the Type pop-up menu and name the file hot2.pic (see fig. 5.2).

Figure 5.2
You will create several variations of the flaming letters.

12.   Repeat for hot3.pic and hot4.pic.

13.   Select the entire image.

14.   Choose Filter, KPT, Texture Explorer again.

15.   Click on one of the tiles that looks similar to the one in the middle and choose OK.

16.   Choose File, Save As. Choose PICT from the Type pop-up menu and name the file fire.pic.

Making the Movie

Now you return to Director.

1.   Create a new file.

2.   Choose File, Movie Info and set the default palette to System-Windows.

3.   Choose File, Preferences. Set the stage size to 64×20 and the stage location Top to 22.

4.   Import the hot1–4.pic files and the fire.pic.

5.   Option-drag (Alt-drag in Windows) the four hotx.pic files into the score in frame 1, channel 1.

6.   Select the Background Transparent ink.

Note   In many cases, you have to reorder the sequence of the hot pic files to get them to look the most like fire. If you are using the sample files provided, for example, we recommend the sequence 4-2-3-1.

7. Copy the four sprites and paste them in frames 5–8 of channel 1.

8. Repeat with frames 9–12 and so on, until you have filled the channel to frame 32.

9. Save the file in the Ch05 directory as hot.dir.

Now you have the basic opening sequence. But it is still somewhat uninteresting—there is no climax. In the following steps you create one by making the fire appear to spread from the *O* to the rest of the stage and then burn out.

Warning

The following steps highlight some fairly funky uses of Director's paint window. Even if you decide to follow the directions, it might still benefit you to look at the example files provided.

1. Open one of the hot.pic files in the paint window by double-clicking on it.

2. Using the marquee tool, select the *O* and copy it.

3. Select the *O* and Command-click (Control-click in Windows) on it to magnify the image.

4. Using the lasso tool, select a pointed shape that is part of the *O* and Option-drag it up and to the left. Option-dragging drags a copy of the selection.

5. Select a roughly circular portion of the *O* and Option-drag it into the middle of the *O*. Your cast member should look something like figure 5.3 when magnified.

6. Choose Cast, Duplicate Cast Member to make a duplicate of the cast member. The duplicate will then be selected and magnified.

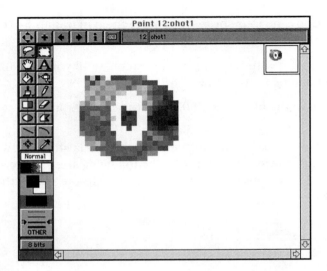

Figure 5.3
The magnified image of the first burning *O*.

7. Fill in the rest of the middle of the *O* by either copying little bits of the rest of the *O* or by using the pencil tool to use random shades of orange from the rest of the image.

Tip   Clicking with the Control key held down (the right mouse button in Windows) turns the pencil tool into an eyedropper, which makes it easy to grab the colors from other parts of the image.

Enlarge the pointed shape in the same fashion.

8. Choose Cast, Duplicate Cast Member to make a duplicate of the cast member. The duplicate will then be selected and magnified.

9. Enlarge the pointed shape by either copying little bits of the rest of the *O* or by using the pencil tool to use random shades of orange from the rest of the image.

10. Repeat the last two steps twice more, making the pointed shape wider as well as longer.

Your cast should now look approximately like figure 5.4.

Figure 5.4

The cast after creating the five burning *O*s.

11. Option-drag (Alt-drag in Windows) all the burning *O*s into frame 24, channel 5 (they will extend to frame 28).

12. Making sure they all stay selected and that the playback head is at frame 24, position the *O*s so that they match the *O* in *HOT*.

For fine adjustments, the best method is to deselect the sprite, then rock back and forth between the frame containing the sprite and an adjacent one. When the sprite is correctly positioned, you should see no difference between the two frames.

Tip

Play the file and save it. The *O* should burn satisfactorily now, but the fire doesn't spread to the rest of the stage. You do that in the following steps.

Importing files maskrt.pic, masklft.pic, and masktop.pic replaces the next seven steps.

Shortcut

1. Open the paint window. Click on the + button for a new cast member.

2. Draw a rectangle the same color as the stage background, at least as tall as the stage and at least two-thirds as wide.

3. Set the foreground color to white.

4. With the pencil tool, carve out flame-like shapes from the left side of the object, so that magnified, it looks like figure 5.5.

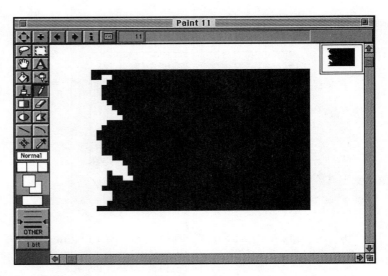

Figure 5.5
The right mask cast member, magnified.

5. Repeat steps 1–4, except carve out the shapes on the right side of the object.

6. Draw a third rectangle, at least 150 percent as tall as the movie stage and at least as wide.

7. Carve out yet more flames, this time on the bottom of the rectangle. Make sure you carve out only the bottom third of the rectangle.

Your cast should now look like figure 5.6.

You now need to use the masks to spread the fire. This is where the fire.pic cast member comes in.

1. Move the sprites in frames 29–32, channel 1 to channel 4.

2. Drag the fire.pic cast member into frame 29, channel 1.

Figure 5.6
The three mask cast members enable the fire to grow and consume the whole stage before dwindling to nothing.

3. Select frames 29–40 of channel 1. Choose Score, In-Between Linear. The In-Between Linear command interpolates the sprite position and size between the beginning and end of the selection in a linear manner. If there is no sprite in the end position, however, it simply copies the sprite. The In-Between Special command enables you to interpolate more than just the position and the size of the sprite, as well as create curved interpolations.

4. With the playback head at frame 29, drag the maskrt cast member onto the stage so that it is just to the right of the *O* and covers the stage from top to bottom.

5. Check that the maskrt sprite is in channel 2 of the score and move it there if not.

6. Give it Background Transparent ink.

Tip

Any cast member dragged onto the stage or into the score by default will have the same ink as was last applied. So now that you have given the first sprite Background Transparent ink, the rest of the sprites will have the same ink unless you change it.

7. Drag the masklft cast member onto the stage so that it is just to the left of the *O*. Make sure it is in channel 3.

8. Select frame 29, channels 2 and 3, and Option-drag (Alt-drag in Windows) them to frame 33.

9. Move the masks to their respective edges of the stage.

10. Select frames 29–33, channels 2 and 3, and choose Score, In-Between.

Play the movie. The fire should now build. Your score should look like figure 5.7, and when the playback head is at frame 30, the stage should look something like the figure as well.

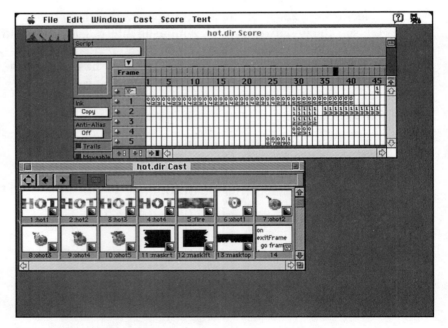

Figure 5.7
The fire builds at the end of the movie to add a climax.

The following steps make the fire dwindle at the end.

1. Move the playback head to frame 35. Drag the masktop cast member into the score in channel 2.

2. Move it on the stage so that it is at the very top of the stage.

3. Option-drag (Alt-drag in Windows) the sprite to frame 40, channel 2 of the score.

4. On the stage, move the sprite down so it covers the whole stage.

5. Select frames 35–45, channel 2 and choose Score, In-Between Linear.

6. In the script channel of frame 45, type the following script:

```
on exitFrame
      go the frame
end exitFrame
```

7. Select all frames in channels 2 and 3. Open the tools window and change the foreground color chip to 30 percent gray or the same gray used in the background of channel 1, frames 1–29.

The movie is now done; save your changes. Figure 5.8 shows the score of the finished movie.

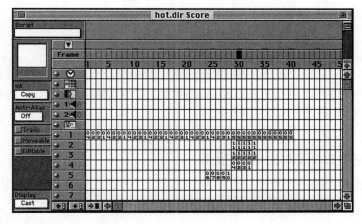

Figure 5.8

The finished score of the hot.dir movie.

Compressing and Embedding the Movie

1. Drag the movie onto Afterburner.

2. Save it in the Movies subdirectory of the Ch05 folder as hot.dcr.

3. In your text editor, open the ex5_1.htm file.

4. Before the Area 3 line, put the tag:

    ```
    <embed src="Movies/hot.dcr" width=64 height=20>
    ```

Save the file and open it again in your browser. Play the movie. In the next section, you use Director's inks to create some interesting effects.

EXAMPLE 5-2:

New! Movie

This movie highlights two of the most powerful weapons in a Shockwave developer's arsenal: colored 1-bit cast members and ink effects.

Director enables you to colorize 1-bit PICT files on the fly, which means you can get 256 different cast members for the price of one!

Director offers 18 different inks, which govern the way Director draws cast members on the screen. These can add a tremendous number of visual effects to your movies, again without increasing download size. The New! movie in this example is yet another attention-getter that demonstrates these techniques.

Creating the Effect

For this movie, we used Adobe Premiere to create a rippling word.

Shortcut

Use the files new01.pic to new20.pic in the news subdirectory of the Ch05\Src folder.

1. Open Premiere. Choose File, New, New Project. Choose the 160×120 preset.

2. Choose Make, Output Options.

3. Deselect the Audio checkbox and the 4:3 Aspect Ratio checkbox.

4. Set the dimensions to 80×45.

5. Set the second pop-up menu to Numbered PICT files. The top should now read `output work area as numbered PICT files`. Choose OK.

6. Choose Make, Compression Options.

7. In the Compression pop-up, select None.

8. In the Frames Per Second text box, type `10`.

9. Choose File, Import File and open file new.pic in the Ch05\Src folder.

10. Drag the clip into the Premiere Timeline and extend it, if necessary, so that the duration is two seconds.

11. Select the clip and choose Clip, Filters.

12. In the Available scroll box, double-click on the ripple filter.

13. In the Ripple Settings dialog box, slide the rate and intensity sliders for the Vertical settings all the way to the left, then choose OK. Figure 5.9 shows the settings.

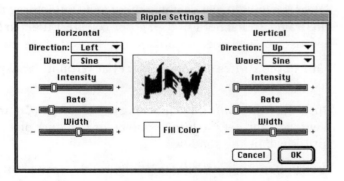

Figure 5.9
The ripple settings for this effect.

14. Choose Make, Movie. Create a new directory called myrip, and save the file as newrip.pic. This will generate 20 pict files.

Making the Movie

Now you begin working in Director.

1. Choose File, Movie Info and set the default palette to System-Win.

2. Choose File, Preferences and set the stage size to 80×45.

3. Choose File, Import, then navigate to the myrip folder and choose Import All to import the 20 newrip pict files.

4. Import the original pict file, new.pic, which is in the Ch05\Src folder.

5. Open the control panel. On the color chip on the lower right of the panel, select black. This sets the stage background color to black.

6. Save the file in the Ch05 folder as new.dir.

7. Select all the cast members and choose Cast, Transform Bitmap to display the Transform Bitmap dialog box. Select 1 Bit in the Color Depth drop-down list, choose OK, and then OK the warning message.

8. Select the first 20 pict cast members and Option-drag them into frame 2, channel 1 of the score. You start them in frame 2 because you will need a transition at the end of the movie.

9. With all the sprites selected, select Background Transparent ink.

10. Open the tool window by choosing Command+7 (Control+7 in Windows) and set the foreground color to a dark blue. These sprites will be the shadow.

11. Now Option-drag (Alt-drag in Windows) the sprites to channel 2.

12. In the tool window, select a lighter blue.

13. Press the left-arrow key twice and the up-arrow key twice. This moves the sprites two pixels up and two pixels to the left.

The convention for both Macintosh and Windows is to shade everything as if the light were coming from the upper left. If you examine a button on either platform, you will notice that the top and left edges are lighter than the face, and the bottom and right edges are darker. Many designers make the mistake of lighting from another angle (the top right is the most common example), which can look very strange. Unless you have a reason for doing it otherwise, we recommend following this convention.

Tip

Play the movie. Save it as new.dir in the Ch05 folder.

Copy all the sprites and paste them into frames 22–41. Repeat the paste in frames 42, 62, 82, 102, and 122.

Now you have the basic text for the movie. Of course, since you are going to all this effort to emphasize the newness of this item, you should emphasize it with an exclamation point.

1. Import the file exclam.pic from the Ch05 folder.

2. Open the cast member in the paint window.

3. Choose Cast, Duplicate Cast Member.

4. Double-click on the marquee tool to select the entire bitmap.

5. Select Effects, Rotate Right.

6. Repeat steps 3–5 twice.

You should now have four exclamation-point cast members, at 90-degree increments.

7. Select all four exclamation-point cast members and choose Cast, Transform Bitmap.

8. Set the color depth to 1 Bit, choose OK, and OK the warning message. See figure 5.10 for the cast at this point.

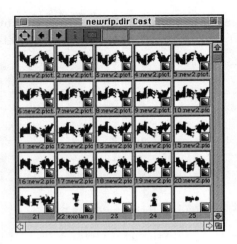

Figure 5.10

The cast after duplicating and rotating the exclamation point.

Tip

We changed the color depth of the exclamation point *after* rotating it because none of the effects work for 1-bit cast members.

9. Set the playback head to frame 28. Drag the first exclamation-point cast member onto the right edge of the stage.

10. In the tool palette, set the color to dark green.

11. In the score, make sure the sprite is in channel 3.

12. Option-drag (Alt-drag in Windows) the sprite from channel 3 to 4.

13. In the tool palette, set the color to a light green.

14. Use the arrow keys to move the sprite in channel 4 two pixels up and two to the left.

15. Select the sprites in both channels 3 and 4. Option-drag (Alt-drag in Windows) them to frame 36.

16. On the stage, drag the sprites so that they are over the first vertical stroke of the *W* (see fig. 5.11, a).

Figure 5.11
The last three keyframes of the bouncing exclamation point.

17. Option-drag (Alt-drag in Windows) the sprites to frame 44.

18. On the stage, drag the sprites so that they are over the middle of the *N* (see fig. 5.11, b).

19. Option-drag (Alt-drag in Windows) the sprites to frame 51.

20. Drag the sprites to the left edge of the stage (see fig. 5.11, c).

21. Select frames 28–51, channels 3 and 4 in the score.

22. Select Score, In-Between Special.

23. Set the path slider to halfway between the center and the right end of the bar.

24. Choose OK.

In-Between Special gives you rudimentary nonlinear motion. In this case, we use it to provide smoother motion on the bouncing exclamation point.

Tip

25. Option-drag the two sprites in frame 51, channels 3 and 4 to frame 62.

26. In the cast, select the upside-down exclamation point. Choose Score, Switch Cast Members. This replaces the castmember(s) of the selected sprite(s) with the castmember selected in the cast window.

The Switch Cast Members command changes the cast of a sprite without changing any of the other characteristics of that sprite.

Note

27. Switch to the score window. With the two sprites still selected, move them so they are almost off the top edge of the stage over the first vertical stroke of the *W*.

28. In the score, Option-drag the sprites to frame 74.

29. Move them straight down on the stage so they are almost off the bottom edge.

30. Select frames 62–74, channels 3 and 4 and choose Score, In-Between Linear.

31. Select the four exclamation-point cast members and Option-drag them into the score (anywhere).

32. In the tool window, select the same color as you used for the text shadow on NEW.

33. Option-drag the four sprites into the next higher channel. Select the color you used for the foreground NEW text.

34. Select the sprites in both channels and drag them into an open slot in the cast. You now are creating a film loop. Name the loop "spin blue."

 Note

Film loops are encapsulated bits of score; however, they don't always act in the expected manner. You cannot set the ink or color of film loops—they take their ink and color from the settings of the sprites that make them up. If you look at them in the cast while you are not actually playing the movie, they will always show the first cast member in the loop. It is a good idea to turn off the sound on the film loop in the cast info (Control-click on the Mac or right-click in Windows), because sometimes a film loop with sound checked will override the sound playing in the sound channel, even if it doesn't exist.

35. Select the four exclamation point sprites in channels 3 and 4. Color the sprites in channel 3 dark red and the sprites in channel 4 bright red.

36. Drag all eight sprites into the cast member. Name the resulting film loop "Spin Red."

37. Select the eight sprites in the score and press the backspace key.

38. Drag the "spin blue" film loop into the score at frame 112, channel 4 and position the sprite at the top of the stage directly above the *N*.

39. Option-drag the sprite to frame 125 and on the stage move it so that it is over the middle of the *W*, with the dot part of the exclamation point slightly overlapping the *W*.

40. Option-drag the sprite in the score again to 139 and on the stage drag it straight down so that it is nearly off the bottom edge of the stage.

41. Select frames 112–139 of channel 4 of the score and choose Score, In-Between Linear.

42. Move the playback head back to frame 110 and play the movie. Note that the sprite spins, although it did not while you were positioning it.

Now you add some geometric shapes to the movie for visual interest.

1. In the paint window, draw a cast member with four black regularly spaced parallel vertical lines, roughly 90 pixels long and approximately 5 pixels apart, as shown in figure 5.12.

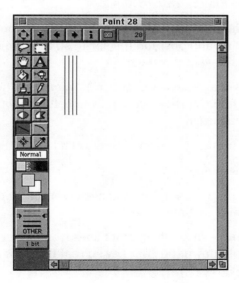

Figure 5.12

Adding geometric shapes adds visual interest to the movie.

Tip You can draw horizontal, vertical, or 45-degree angle lines by holding down the Shift key while you draw.

2. Drag the cast member into frame 9, channel 6 of the score and move it vertically so that the bottom edge of the lines is at the top of the stage.

3. In the score, select Reverse ink.

4. Option-drag the sprite in the score to frame 23.

5. Move the sprite vertically so that the top edge of the lines is at the bottom of the stage.

6. Select frames 9–23 and select Score, In-Between Linear.

7. Save the file.

8. Select the cast member that consists of four vertical lines. Choose Cast, Duplicate.

9. Open the duplicate in the paint window. Double-click on the marquee tool to select the cast member.

10. Choose Effects, Rotate Right.

11. Drag the cast member into the score in frame 47, channel 7 of the score, and position the sprite so that the right edge is at the left edge of the stage.

12. Option-drag the cast member to frame 60. Choose Score, Sprite Info. Set the Location from Left Edge of Stage to 80 and choose OK.

13. Select frames 17–60 and In-Between Linear.

Now, create a new shape.

14. Open the paint window and click on the + button to create a new paint cast member.

15. Draw three diagonal parallel lines from upper right to lower left. Hold down the Shift key so that the lines are constrained to 45 degrees.

16. Drag the new cast member into frame 70, channel 7 of the score.

17. Drag the sprite to the right half of the stage and down to the bottom edge.

18. Option-drag the sprite in the score to frame 92.

19. Drag the sprite to the upper left corner of the stage.

20. Select frames 70–92 and choose Score, In-Between Linear.

21. Select the horizontal lines cast member and drag to frame 95, channel 7. Position it so that it is just off the center left of the stage.

22. Option-drag this cast member to frame 111 of the same channel. Position it so that it is just off the center right of the stage.

23. Select frames 95–111 of channel 7 and select Score, In-Between Linear.

24. Select the vertical lines cast member and drag to frame 95, channel 8.

25. Option-drag this cast member to frame 112 of the same channel. Position it so that it is just off the center top of the stage.

26. Select frames 95–112, channel 8 and select Score, In-Between Linear. The horizontal and vertical lines should cross at center.

27. Drag the horizontal lines cast member into frame 133, channel 6 and another into frame 133, channel 7. Position the first cast member in the top half of the stage and the second cast member in the bottom half so that it looks like eight evenly spaced lines.

28. Select both sprites and choose Score, Sprite Info. Set the distance from left edge of stage to minus the width of the sprites. (If the sprite is 90 pixels wide, set the distance to –90.)

29. Option-drag the sprites to frame 158.

30. Choose Score, Sprite Info and set the distance from left edge of stage to 80.

31. Select frames 133–158 in channels 6 and 7, and choose Score, In-Between Linear.

32. Select the sprites in frames 70–92, channel 7. Option-drag them to frame 138, channel 9.

33. With the sprites selected, choose Score, Reverse Sequence. This will make the lines go from the top left to bottom right.

34. Save the file.

35. Select the sequence of frames 122–141, channels 1 and 2. Option-drag them to frame 142.

36. Step along the score until the back edge of the horizontal lines is even with the back edge of the text. Delete the text sprites after that.

37. Option-drag the last remaining text sprites (in both channels 1 and 2) until they are at the last frame in which the horizontal lines are visible (which should be the second-to-last frame containing the line sprites).

38. Select the last frame of the sequence and the one you just added and choose Score, In-Between Linear.

39. Now you must manually replace the new sprites with the appropriate ones from the ripple sequence.

40. Save the file. Your score should look something like figure 5.13.

41. Drag the horizontal-line cast member into frame 150, channel 4. Select Reverse ink. Position it so the third line down is at the bottom of the stage, and just off the left edge of the stage.

42. Option-drag the sprite to frame 183.

43. Use Sprite info to set the distance from left edge of stage to 80.

44. Select frames 150-183, channel 4 and choose Score, In-Between Linear.

45. Drag the non-rippled NEW cast member into frame 152, channel 5.

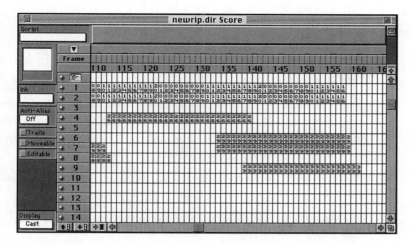

Figure 5.13
The score prior to adding the finale.

46. Drag it to the upper left corner of the stage.

47. Select Background Transparent ink. Color it the same bright red you used for the foreground of the "spin red" film loop.

48. Option-drag the sprite to frame 161. Position it so the bottom edge is resting just on the top line of the horizontal lines and the bottom right corner of the *W* is at the tip of the top line.

49. Select frames 152–201 of channel 5. Choose Score, In-Between Linear.

50. Option-drag the selection into the same frames of channel 3.

51. Select the same dark red you used as the background color of the "spin red" film loop.

52. Press the right-arrow key twice and the down-arrow key twice. Now the sprites in channel 3 are a shadow.

53. Drag the "spin red" film loop into frame 180, channel 6 of the score. Drag it just off the bottom of the stage at the horizontal center.

54. Option-drag the sprite in the score to frame 194. Position it so that it looks like it goes with the text.

55. Select frames 180–199, channel 6 and choose Score, In-Between Linear.

56. Drag the upright exclamation-point cast member onto frame 199, channel 7 of the score. Color it the bright red you are using as the foreground color. Make sure that the ink setting for the sprite is Background Transparent.

57. Position it so that it exactly overlaps the foreground part of the film loop.

58. Option-drag it into channel 6 of the same frame. This will overwrite the film loop.

59. Color the background red and press the right-arrow key twice and the down-arrow key twice.

60. Select channels 6 and 7, frames 199–201 and choose Score, In-Between Linear.

61. In the script channel of frame 201, click on the script bar and type the following script:

```
on exitFrame
     go the frame
end exitFrame
```

Save and play the movie. Looks good, doesn't it? Now there is one more addition, just for fun.

1. Select frames 168–175 of channel 3.

2. Select Reverse ink.

3. Repeat for the same frames of channel 5.

4. Play that section of the movie.

Note

The preceding effect is achieved because both sprites have Reverse ink; they cancel each other out where they overlap. So, what you see is the parts where they don't overlap. We will be doing some even more crazy things with inks later on.

Compressing and Embedding the File

1. Drag the file onto Afterburner.

2. Save it as new.dcr in the Ch05/Movies folder.

3. Open the ex5_2.htm file.

4. Change the embed tag you added in example 5:1 to read:
   ```
   <embed src="Movies/new.dcr" width=80 height=45>.
   ```

View the file, but be careful—it has been known to be somewhat hypnotic.

In the next chapter, you begin to explore something that is a large part of Shockwave work: animating logos. You use the techniques you have learned so far—along with new ones—to explore one kind of task in depth.

PART III

Additional Techniques

CHAPTER 6

Control Panels and Simple Buttons

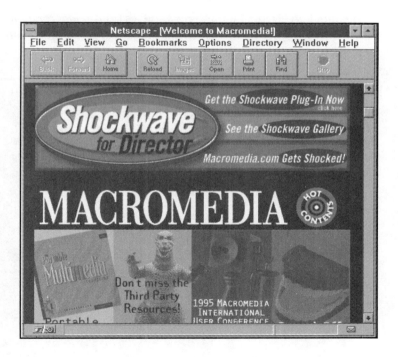

O ne of the major uses for Shockwave is control panels and buttons that jump to another page. In this chapter, you explore one of Shockwave's Network Lingo Extensions, GoToNetPage, which makes these things possible.

EXAMPLE 6-1:

Shocked by InfraRed

Shocked by InfraRed is the movie we put on home pages that we shock. It consists of a graphic that initially is inert. When the user moves the cursor over the graphic, however, lightning strikes repeatedly until the mouse is off the stage, at which time there is a crash of thunder. When clicked on, the movie sends the user to our home page.

The Shocked by InfraRed movie appears on the *Macromedia Shockwave for Director User's Guide* CD-ROM as shkir.dir. A sample frame from the movie is shown in figure 6.1.

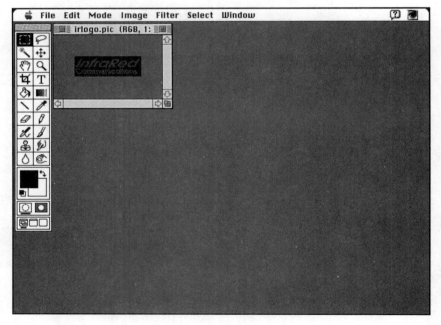

Figure 6.1

A frame from the Shocked by InfraRed movie.

To create the Shocked by InfraRed movie, you'll need to create the logo in Photoshop, edit the logo in Director, create the lightning bolt in Photoshop, and add the thunder sounds before you add the interactivity that makes it come together.

Creating the Logo

The first step in making the Shocked by InfraRed movie is to create the *Shocked by* logo. You begin working in Photoshop.

1. Open the EPS outline of the InfraRed logo, found on the book's CD as irlogo.eps in the Ch06 directory. Select Image, Size, and size the logo so that the vertical dimension is 30 pixels.

2. Set the foreground color to blue and the background to black; select a blue that is available in the system palette to avoid dithering.

3. Choose Image, Canvas Size and set the canvas size to be 208×34 and position the logo center right of the canvas.

The vertical size is somewhat arbitrary, but Director requires the horizontal dimension of the movie to be divisible by 16 for performance reasons.

Note

4. Using the Photoshop text tool, type `Shocked` in 24-point TemplateGothic Bold (or the font of your choice), with the italic box checked to give a slightly more dynamic look to the text (see fig. 6.2).

You should type the text in Photoshop for two reasons. First, the text needs to be bitmapped because you cannot expect the user to have an obscure font such as TemplateGothic Bold. And second, Photoshop's antialiasing gives the text a smoother look.

Tip

5. Change the foreground color to white.

6. Type `by` in the same font, only in 12 point. Center it vertically.

7. Save the file as a 16-bit pict with the file name By.pct.

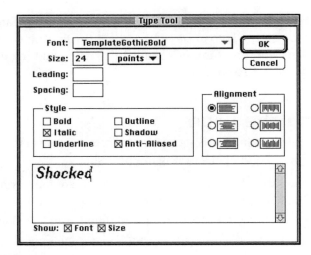

Figure 6.2
Italic is used for the Shocked logo for a more dynamic look.

Note

You do not dither it here, but in Director, because Photoshop does not have a Windows System Palette built in.

Editing the Logo

Next, you'll import the file into Director and edit the logo. Before you do so, however, if you are working on a Macintosh, make sure your monitor control panel is set to 256 colors so that the cast member will be an 8-bit bitmap.

Note

On the Macintosh, Director converts cast members to the current color depth of the primary monitor (the one with the menu bar). Because most users have only 256 color (8-bit) displays, and because 16- or 32-bit cast members take much longer to download, it is advisable to work in 256 colors.

1. In Director, choose File, Preferences to display the Preferences dialog box. Set the stage size to 208×34.

2. Choose File, Movie Info and set the default palette to System-Windows.

3. Choose File, Import to import the By.pct file. This automatically dithers the image to the current palette, which is the Windows System Palette.

4. Drag the file from the cast to frame 1, channel 1 of the score.

Note

> By dragging it into the score, the image is automatically centered on the stage.

5. Select the first 25 frames of channel 1 in the score.

6. Choose Score, In-Between Linear or press Command+B (Control+B in Windows).

You now have the background for the entire movie, as shown in figure 6.3. Now you need to make a mask so that the lightning will appear to strike through the *o* of the word *Shocked*.

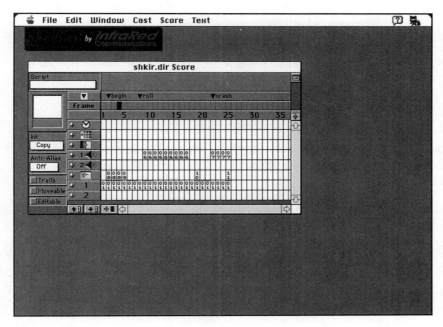

Figure 6.3
The background for the entire Shocked by InfraRed movie.

7. Double-click on the image in the cast. This displays the paint window to edit that cast member.

8. With the marquee tool, select the top third of the *o* in *Shocked*. Choose Edit, Copy.

9. Click on the + button in the paint window toolbar for a new cast member. Choose Edit, Paste to paste the top of the *o*.

10. Drag the cast member into channel 3, frame 1 of the score. This leaves a channel in the score for the lightning bolt.

11. Select Background Transparent ink for the sprite.

12. In the tool palette, change the background color to black.

The combination of the last two steps will make the color black on the sprite transparent.

13. Using a combination of the mouse and the arrow keys, position the sprite so it exactly overlays the equivalent part of the background image.

14. Highlight frames 1–25, channel 3 and select Score, In-Between Linear to extend the sprite to the end of the movie.

Creating the Lightning Bolt

So far you have created and edited the *Shocked by* logo. With this logo behind you, your next task is to create the lightning bolt. You'll begin in Director.

1. Open the paint window and click on the + button for a new paint cast member. Set the foreground color to black.

2. Draw a lightning bolt, approximately 10×24 pixels (see fig. 6.4).

3. Select Cast, Transform Bitmap. Select 1 Bit in the colordepth pop-up to set the color depth of the lightning bolt.

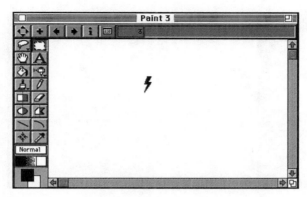

Figure 6.4

The drawn lightning bolt, from which you'll make two copies.

Double-clicking on the colordepth indicator below the paint window tool palette will also display the Transform Bitmap dialog box.   Tip

4. Choose OK, then choose OK to dismiss the warning message.

5. Choose Cast, Duplicate Cast twice to copy the lightning bolt twice.

6. Click on the back-arrow button in the window toolbar.

You are now editing the second of three copies of the lightning bolt.

7. Using the lasso or the marquee tool, select the bottom third of the lightning bolt, then press Del to clear that portion of the bitmap (see fig. 6.5).

8. Click on the forward-arrow button in the window toolbar to highlight the third lightning bolt.

9. Select the bottom two-thirds of that lightning bolt and press Del to clear that portion of the bitmap. You now have a progression of the lightning bolt striking, as shown in figure 6.6.

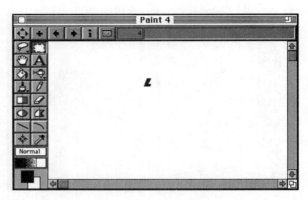

Figure 6.5
Delete the bottom portion of the lightning bolt.

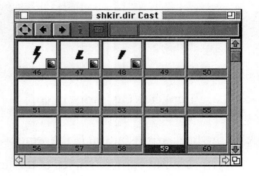

Figure 6.6
The lightning bolt strikes in three stages.

10. Drag the full lightning bolt into frame 8, channel 2 of the score. In the tool palette, set the foreground color to yellow.

11. On the stage, position the bolt so that it looks like it is striking through the *o* in *Shocked* (see fig. 6.7).

12. Select frames 8–17, channel 2, then choose Score, In-Between Linear to extend the sprite across all the frames. Set the foreground color to yellow.

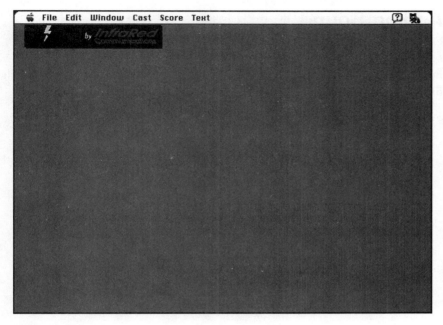

Figure 6.7
Position the bolt so that it strikes through the *o* in *Shocked*.

13. Select frames 8 and 9, channel 2.

14. Select the one-third lightning bolt in the cast.

15. Choose Score, Switch Cast Members or press Command+E (Control+E in Windows).

16. Select frames 10 and 11, channel 2.

17. Select the two-thirds lightning bolt in the cast.

18. Choose Score, Switch Cast Members or press Command+E (Control+E in Windows).

You now have the basic lightning striking sequence. In the control panel, set the tempo (the second number field) to 25 fps.

Now it's time to add some sound.

Adding Sound

From the Macromedia ClipMedia 1 CD, take the "arc" and "thunder" sounds. Then, open them in SoundEdit 16 and shorten them to approximately $1/4$ and $1/2$ a second, respectively. Add a fadeout to the thunder.aif file, then save them at 8-bit, 11.050 KHz, with the AIF extension.

Switch to Director.

1. Choose File, Import and import both sound files you just created.

2. Drag arc.aif in sound frame 8, channel 1.

3. Select frames 8–17 of that channel.

4. Choose Score, In-Between Linear.

5. Drag thunder.aif into sound frame 22, channel 1.

6. Select frames 22–25 of that channel.

7. Choose Score, In-Between Linear.

Play the file. The file will buzz, then there will be a crash.

Adding Interactivity

Now it's time to add interactivity. You make the lightning bolt strike while the mouse is over the movie, and the thunder crash when the mouse leaves it.

First, you need to mark the sections. Drag a marker out to frame 2 and title it "begin," drag a marker out to frame 8 and title it "roll," then drag a marker out to frame 22 and title it "crash."

Next, you want to make the lightning strike when the mouse is over the movie.

1. Click in the script channel in frame 2.

2. Click the script bar on the top of the score window.

3. In the script window, type the following script:

```
on exitFrame
     if rollover(1) then go "roll"
end exitFrame
```

4. Close the script window.

A rollover function returns TRUE if the mouse is over the tested sprite. In this case, you want the function to be true if the mouse is over the movie at all, so you test for the background sprite, which is in channel 1. Because the section with lightning striking begins at the marker "roll," that's where you go.

Note

5. Select frames 3 and 4 in the script window and choose the script you just created from the script pop-up.

6. Click in the script channel in frame 5.

7. Click on the script bar on the top of the score window.

8. In the script window, type the following script:

```
on exitFrame
     if rollover(1) then go "roll"
     else go "begin"
end exitFrame
```

9. Close the script window.

This does the same thing as the first script with the addition of going back to the beginning of the loop if the mouse is not over the movie.

10. Click in the script channel in frame 19.

11. Click the script bar on the top of the score window. In the script window, type the following script:

```
on exitFrame
     if rollover(1) then go "roll"
     else go "crash"
end exitFrame
```

12. Close the script window.

While the mouse is over the movie, you want to make sure the lightning keeps striking repeatedly, so at the end of the strike you need to go again to the beginning of the strike sequence if the mouse is still over the movie. If the mouse is no longer over the movie, you need to go to the thunder section, which starts at marker "crash."

13. Click in the script channel in frame 25.

14. Click the script bar on the top of the score window. In the script window, type the following script:

```
on exitFrame
      if soundBusy(1) then go the frame
      else go "begin"
end exitFrame
```

15. Close the script window.

The soundBusy function tests to see if there is a sound playing in the tested channel. You use it here because you don't want to cut off the thunder sound prematurely. This script loops on the last frame until the sound is done, at which point it goes back to the beginning of the movie.

The final thing you need to do is make the movie do something when a user clicks on it. In the spirit of shameless self-promotion, we made this script go to our home page. Because the background sprite covers the whole stage, we gave it a cast sprite, which will always be active.

1. In the cast window, select the background image.

2. Click on the script button in the window tool bar.

3. In the script window, type the following script:

```
on mouseUp
  goToNetPage("http://www.eline.com/Infrared/Shocked"
end
```

4. Close the script window.

The movie is now finished.

Embedding the Movie

You now need to embed the movie in the HTML page.

1. Drag the movie onto Afterburner. Save it as shkir.dcr in the Ch06/Movies folder.

2. Open the ex6_1.htm file in your text editor. At the bottom of the file, just before the **</body>** tag, add the lines:

```
<center>
<embed src="Movies/shkir.dcr" height=34 width=208>
</center>
```

Open the file in your browser. Clicking on the movie should send you to our home page.

> Another very common use for Shockwave is shameless self-promotion, as in the preceding example. **Tip**

In example 6-2, you explore a more complex use of the GoToNetPage command.

<u>EXAMPLE 6-2:</u>

Simple Control Panel

Possibly the most common use for image maps on the World Wide Web is navigation. You never really know, though, when you are about to click on a button that'll do something. One of the advantages of Shockwave is that you can provide the user with instant feedback.

In this movie you'll use the rollover technique that we used in the preceding example to provide feedback for a control panel.

Creating the Art in Photoshop

1. Open Photoshop. Select File, New. In the Image Size section, specify 60×30 pixels and set the mode to RGB Color. Choose OK.

2. Set the foreground color to red. Using the paint bucket tool, fill the entire image.

3. Switch the red to the background color, and set the foreground color to black.

4. Type **Home** in the font of your choice. This example uses 16-point Helvetica Black, as shown in figure 6.8.

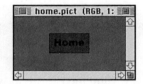

Figure 6.8
The home button uses Helvetica Black for a strong, clear font.

5. Save the file as home.pic, choosing 16 bits in the colordepth dialog box when it appears.

6. Repeat the preceding steps four times, substituting the words "Clients," "Fun," "Info," and "News."

7. Quit Photoshop.

Laying Out the Art in Director

Before you add interactivity, you need to lay out the buttons in Director.

1. Open Director. Choose File, Movie Info and set the default palette to System-Windows.

2. Choose File, Preferences and set the stage size to 336×40.

3. In the control panel, set the stage color to black.

4. Choose File, Import. Navigate to the Ch06/Pics directory and choose Import All.

5. Drag the home.pic cast member onto the stage and position it approximately 5 pixels from the left edge, 5 pixels from the top. Make sure the sprite is in frame 1, channel 1.

6. Drag the news.pic cast member onto the stage and position it approximately 7 pixels to the right of the home.pic file. The sprite should be in frame 1, channel 2.

7. Repeat with the clients, info, and fun picts. They should be in channels 1–5, frame 1. Select frames 1–10 of all five channels and choose Score, In-Between Linear.

Your stage, cast, and score should look like figure 6.9.

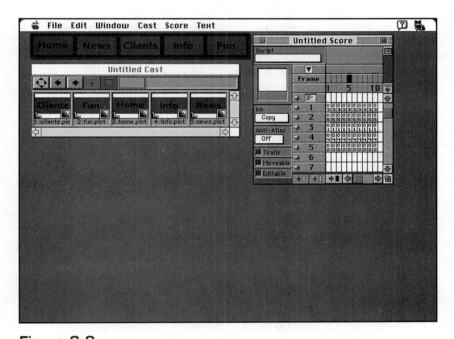

Figure 6.9
The movie before you add actual function.

8. Save the file in the Ch06 folder as panel.dir.

9. In the tool palette, select the unfilled rectangle tool. Set the foreground color to blue and the line width to 2 pixels.

10. Draw a rectangle around one of the buttons. This will be the highlight rectangle that appears when the mouse is over an active button.

11. In the score, drag the rectangle to frame 1, channel 10.

12. Choose Score, Sprite Info and set the Distance from Left Edge of Stage to −100.

Note

You move the sprite off the stage because you will be animating it with Lingo; the sprite should be out of the way until it is needed.

Adding Functionality

Now it is time to make the movie actually do something. You will make the blue square highlight the button the mouse is currently over.

1. In the script channel of frame 1, type the following script:

```
on exitFrame
  puppetSprite 10, TRUE
end
```

Note

The puppetSprite command causes the sprite to ignore the score and be controllable by Lingo. You need to puppetSprite the sprite now because you want to control the position of the sprite with Lingo. Also note that once a sprite is puppeted, it does not need to appear in the score anymore. If this were a more complicated movie, though, it would be advisable to put the sprite in the score all the way through to avoid inadvertently putting another sprite in that channel.

2. In the cast window, select an empty cast member, and choose Window, Script. An empty movie script window will appear. In it you will add the functionality to actually check to see if the mouse is over one of the buttons, and if so, to highlight that button.

3. Type the following script:

```
on checkFrame
  repeat with i = 1 to 5
    if rollover(i) then
      set the rect of sprite 10 to the rect of sprite i
```

```
        exit
      end if
    end repeat
    set the locH of sprite 10 to -100
  end
```

In this script, we repeat for each button sprite checking to see if the mouse is over the sprite. If it is, the script sets the rect of the highlight sprite (see below) to surround the button, then exits the handler, since there is no reason to repeat the check for the other sprites if the mouse is already over one. Finally, if the script finishes the repeat loop and the mouse is not over any button, the script moves the highlight off the stage.

Setting the rect of a sprite to the rect of another sprite makes the first sprite's vertical and horizontal dimensions the same as the second's. You can do this in this example because all the sprites are rectangles.

Now, to invoke the checkFrame handler, you need to put in a score script.

4. Select the script channel in frames 2–9.

5. Click on the script bar and type the following script:

```
on exitFrame
  checkFrame
end
```

6. Select the script channel in frame 10 and type the following script:

```
on exitFrame
  checkFrame
  go the frame
end
```

Save and play the movie. Move the mouse over the buttons—they should highlight.

Now, the final step is to make the buttons actually do something.

7. Select the clients.pic cast member and click on the script button in the window toolbar. Type the following script:

```
on mouseUp
  goToNetPage("../clients.htm")
end
```

Note

The GoToNetPage lingo command (and all the network Lingo commands) use the movie's location as their base URL. Because the movie will go in a Movie subdirectory, we need to reference the parent directory.

8. Add `goToNetPage("../fun.htm")` to the fun.pic cast member, and the equivalent to the other three cast members.

9. Save the file. Quit Director.

10. Drag the file onto Afterburner. Name it panel.dcr and save it in the Ch06/Movies folder.

11. With your text editor, open the home.htm file in the Ch06 directory.

12. At the bottom of the page, immediately before the `</body>` tag, embed the movie with the line `<embed src="Movies/panel.dcr" width=332 height=40>`. Add this line to all the htm files in the folder.

Open one of the files in your Web browser. Test the control panel. It will take you from one page to another.

This chapter introduced the GoToNetPage command, which will recur many times throughout this book, and the use of Shockwave for buttons and control panels. In the next chapter, you learn to animate pre-existing logos, a staple of any Shockwave developer's work.

CHAPTER 7

Animated Logos

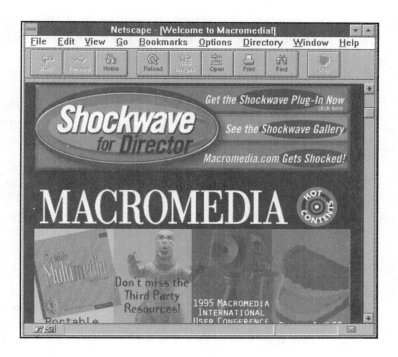

I n this chapter you tackle a more involved design and production challenge: shocking corporate logos. You delve into the shocking of two corporate logos that are being used successfully on the Web. The process of creating the first logo example teaches useful techniques in Photoshop for transforming a single existing logo graphic into a cast of multiple images for use in Director. You then animate the cast, learning more about score window techniques. The end result is a completed Shockwave movie of a complex logo.

In the second logo example, you learn to use Fractal Design Painter to create an original character animation based on an existing company logo. You also learn to add interesting QuickDraw textures and colors without adding much file size. Finally, you examine some advanced ink effects. As we begin this chapter, our point of departure is to pose a very basic question in Shockwave development.

What Makes a Good Animated Logo?

A good animated logo builds on the strengths and design sense already present in the static logo. Animation can make a good logo better and a bad logo worse. If you want to make an animated logo when no static version yet exists, you should first spend time designing a static logo that communicates well without animation.

When shocking an existing static logo, spend time studying its design. Consider its strengths both as a free-standing piece and within a Web page. Try to discover what makes it a good static logo. What gives it character? How do its parts relate to one another? Where is the visual tension and flow? With practice, you can learn how to feel the impulse within the static logo image before you animate. It suggests to you how it "wants" to move.

You can't always know beforehand which combination of movement and sound will unlock the hidden life frozen inside a static logo, however. Create different experimental versions and watch and listen to them. Think about other possibilities and combinations. Try them out. Show these variations to others. How do they see them?

Shocking a logo is more than making it dance around and change. A good shocking can enhance the impact of a logo by creating mood and context. A well-shocked logo is an immersive little world complementing the moving logo with sound and an expanded visual environment. It is not an annoyance on the Web page; on the contrary, it is inviting to watch and adds to the total impact of the page.

EXAMPLE 7-1:

Shocking the Organic Online Logo

Organic Online is a full-service Web provider (to whom we are grateful for giving permission to use their logo as an example in this book). Their logo, shown in figure 7.1, is ripe with animation possibilities.

Figure 7.1
Organic Online's Web page billboard ready to be shocked.

Visualizing the Motion in a Static Logo

First, study the background. Notice that the boundary shape is oval, almost egglike, which suggests fullness or self-containment. The texture is leaflike, breaking into printed circuit patterns here and there suggesting growth and technology. Together, the bounding oval and the textured background is already a perfectly good visual environment for the logo.

Now study the Organic logo shown in figure 7.1. It is formed by the combination of text, the leafy-shaped letter *O,* and a stepped line that connects them and terminates in a punctuation mark. Try reading the logo several times. What paths do your eyes trace as you read it? Toward what areas do your eyes gravitate as you begin and end the reading?

The designers of the static logo did a good job in creating strong lines of eye movement. The strongest line takes your eyes around the leafy *O* which then bridges across the word *ONLINE* and continues right to a hard stop at the small punctuating black circle.

So, without any animation, the image already contains a great deal of motion and tension. It just happens to be the motion of the viewers' eyes that results in visual tension. Our goal in designing a shocked version of Organic's logo is to sense and translate these implied motions to enhance the mood they create to begin with. Using animation built around the natural reading path and rhythm, we are able to invite the viewer to read the image many times and enjoy it each time.

Now is a good time to take a look at our finished version of the Organic logo. Copy the Ch07 folder from the CD to your hard drive. Open the Director file OrgWin.dir from the Ch07/Organic folder. This is the movie we just described, and which you are about to re-create. Play the movie; when you are finished, stop the movie and quit Director.

Preparing the Cast by Decomposing the Original Bitmap

The first step in shocking a logo is gathering visuals for the cast. You will find out that much of the work in shocking an existing logo is simply breaking the logo down and building it back up again.

As is often the case, when we were called upon to shock the Organic logo, the only available artwork was a finished bitmap image embedded in the company's Web page. When shocking a logo it is much preferred to work from the original static source files from the artist or agency who created it, and not from the final image at screen resolution.

The advantages of using the source files are twofold. First, you will often need to manipulate the images by applying scaling, rotation, antialiasing, dithering, and so on. For such procedures, the best results are obtained by working on a high-resolution, full bit-depth original and then later reducing down to screen resolution (72 pixels per inch, 8 bits per pixel).

But the most important reason to go to the source files is to simplify the decomposition of the image. A bitmapped logo posted on the Web is a single composite image made from many layers of images using layers in Adobe Photoshop, or made in dedicated compositing programs such as Specular Collage. Shocking a logo usually requires us to separate the layers of the logo so that they can be animated independently. If you have access to the layered source files, you can easily pull apart the separate layers, yielding a cast of images nearly ready to animate.

We did not have this luxury when shocking Organic's logo. When we captured the Organic logo from the Web, all of its layers were one. Decomposing this image for animation requires stripping the foreground off the background by hand, and simulating the missing background texture obscured by the foreground.

Stripping the Foreground Image

Here you will learn to use Photoshop to strip or isolate the foreground image from the background. This will yield an independent foreground image for importing later into Director. To accomplish this, you use the magic wand tool in Photoshop.

You can skip this section and just use the Org1bit.pct file from the CD-ROM Ch07/Organic folder.

 Shortcut

1. Open the file OrgComp.pic using Photoshop.

2. Double-click on the magic wand in the toolbar. In the magic wand palette, type **0** in the tolerance field and enable the antialiased option.

Tip

The magic wand is a good way to select regions of high contrast such as text. Clicking the magic wand over a spot on a bitmap image automatically makes a selection marquee around a contiguous region of equal or nearly equal brightness. Adjusting the tolerance setting tells the magic wand how much change in image brightness to tolerate. Using a higher tolerance setting will yield a larger selection area.

We suggest mastering the magic wand technique in this exercise, as it is a generally useful tool. Of course there are other techniques in Photoshop to isolate text or solid colored areas. Using Select, Color Range, for example, enables you to automatically marquee a specified color or color range. Try Select, Color Range with the Select Shadows option.

3. Click the magic wand inside the letter *r* of the word *Organic*. This selects a marquee around the letter.

4. While holding down the shift key, click the magic wand inside each of the other letters until the whole phrase *Organic ONLINE* is selected in a marquee.

   Don't worry about selecting the stepped line and the small punctuation circle. You will re-create these separately using lines and circles within Director.

5. To select the leafy-shaped *O*, increase the magic wand tolerance to 50 and shift-click inside the crescent of the *O*.

6. Reduce the tolerance to 25 and shift-click in the leaves until they all are selected.

7. You probably will need to refine the shape of your selection marquee. If the little leaves on the wheat circle are not all selected, for example, you can continue to shift-click with the magic wand until they all are selected. Be prepared to undo your actions; an unlucky clicking of the wand could cause the selection of an unintended region. If this happens, just undo and try a different tolerance setting or click the magic wand on a slightly different spot until you get the desired selection.

   Or, you may have too much area selected, such as an unwanted protrusion from the selection zone. In Photoshop, adding to or removing areas from the selection can be done with the lasso selection tool.

Tip

In Photoshop, the lasso selection tool is used to create and modify an arbitrarily shaped selection marquee. You can use it alone or in combination with the magic wand. With your selection still active, change from the magic wand to the lasso selection tool. To increase the areas of your selection, hold the shift key as you click and trace with the mouse. Similarly, to subtract from your selection just hold the Command key (Control in Windows) as you click and trace with the mouse. Also, the selection mode changes from freehand drawing to polygon drawing when you hold down the option key. In polygon drawing mode, you click to mark each of the vertices of a polygon shaped outline.

8. When you are satisfied that the foreground logo image is properly selected, cut and paste it into a new file. Save it as a pict file.

9. Make a 1-bit version of the image by choosing Mode, Grayscale. Choose OK to discard color information.

10. Choose Mode, Bitmap. Set the Method to 50 percent Threshold.

11. Clean up the bitmap with the brush and/or the pencil tool.

Finally, save the file with a new filename. Use a meaningful filename such as fg1-bit.pic (short for foreground 1-bit). You will import this 1-bit file into Director later.

Simulating the Missing Background Areas

Here you will learn to use Photoshop to simulate or re-create the "invisible" portions of the background, yielding a whole continuous background. To accomplish this, you must patch over the foreground image with bits and pieces from other parts of the background. We use Photoshop's rubber stamp tool to do this.

Shortcut

You can skip this section and just use the OrgBG.pct file from the CD-ROM Ch07/Organic folder.

1. Open the file OrgComp.pic using Photoshop.

2. Choose File, Save As and save it with a new filename. Make sure it is saving in the PICT format. Type a filename that reminds you this is a background (for example, bg.pic) and choose OK.

    Make sure it is saving in 16-bit resolution. It will be reduced to 8-bit depth later in Director.

Note

The rubber stamp tool is not the most simple tool or technique you can use to simulate missing background. It is, however, the most flexible and powerful. You should learn to use it now because it can yield the most natural-looking results, and it is also useful for many other tasks.

A similar but less demanding technique for patching a background is to make an appropriately shaped marquee selection of a source region using the lasso tool, and then copy and paste it over the unwanted portions.

For further control, you can use the Paste Into command. Select a large area of the background and copy it. Then using the lasso tool, marquee the foreground images to be targeted for cover up and choose Edit, Paste Into. This will fill the background only into the target selection area. Before you deselect, you can use the arrow cursor to position the background within the target. Or you can even apply rotation, scaling, and so on.

3. Double-click on the stamp tool.

4. In the Rubber Stamp Options palette, select Normal, 100 percent opacity, and Clone (aligned).

5. In the Brushes palette, choose the 9-pixel brush, which is in the second row, second from the left.

Tip

Using the rubber stamp tool with the Clone (aligned) option is a two-step process and one that requires some practice. First you Option-click (Alt-click in Windows) on an anchor point, and then click on an offset target and paint. Painting this way takes whatever is underneath the anchor point (under the little crosshairs) and transfers that to the target. The offset stays the same until you reset it by Option-clicking (Alt-clicking in Windows) on a new anchor and clicking on a new offset.

The key to doing convincing rubber stamp tool work is knowing where to set the anchor point and offset the target point. Patching a smooth gradient background requires a different technique than patching a geometrically regular texture or a randomly textured background. As usual, keep good backups to revert to as needed and use the trial-and-error method freely. With practice, you can paint over almost any foreground, extend any background, or do even more serious photo doctoring.

6. With the rubber stamp tool, select an anchor point about a half-inch to the left of the wheat circle by Option-clicking (Alt-clicking in Windows).

7. Click on your offset target on the left hemisphere of the wheat circle and paint along the black circle. Notice how the circle gets covered by pixels from underneath the crosshairs.

8. Repeat this process, patiently choosing different anchor points from the background.

When you are satisfied that you have done a convincing job synthesizing a continuous background, save and quit Photoshop. You will import this background image into Director in the next section.

You now have the raw visual material to import into your Director cast.

Importing the Cast into Director and Separating Characters

These are the last steps in preparing the cast for animation. The foreground and background bitmaps are imported into Director, then you further separate the foreground text into its component letters for independent animation. Adding QuickDraw objects such as a circle and three lines will nearly complete the visual elements of the cast.

If you followed along with the last two sections, you should use the two files you created (a 1-bit foreground image and a 16-bit background). If you didn't create your own foreground and background files, just use the ones included in the Ch07/Organic folder of the CD-ROM. For convenience, we will refer to the filenames of these prepared files, but use your own if you made them.

1. Launching the Director application gives you a new file to work with. Save with a new filename. Choose a descriptive filename, such as Organic.dir.

2. Choose File, Movie Info. For the Default Palette setting, select System-Win.

Tip

When making movies for Shockwave, you'll be wise to use the Windows System palette. There are far more Windows machines browsing the Web than any other, so you are vastly reducing the chances of your movie having palette issues when you use the Windows palette.

The palette choice is a very important consideration when you create a new Director movie. Changing palettes later will usually ruin the appearance of any 8-bit cast members. The ultimate fail-safe method against disastrous palette issues is to keep 16-bit or 24-bit source versions of all the PICTs you use in your movies. Then if you ever need to reengineer your Director movie to a different palette, you can just change the default palette and re-import the high color-depth PICTs, and Director will dither them to your new palette.

3. If you are using a Windows machine, skip to step 4. If you are using a Mac, make sure your monitor is set to 8-bit color depth by using the Monitors Control Panel. On a Mac, you can check this within Director by opening the Message window (Command+M) and typing `put the colorDepth` <Return>. If it doesn't respond with `– 8`, then type `set the colorDepth = 8` <Return>.

4. Choose File, Import to display the Import File dialog box. Specify PICT files in the file type list box, then import the following files one-by-one: OrgComp.pic, Org1-bit.pic, and OrgBG.pic.

Note

Director 4.0 Windows only runs in 8-bit color depth, therefore all imported bitmaps are dithered to 8-bit color depth. On a Mac, you need to be aware of the monitor's color depth when importing. In step 4 of this example, you set your monitor to 8-bit before you imported the PICTs into the cast. Therefore, Director changed them all to 8-bit depth automatically. The 1-bit logo and the 16-bit background appear unchanged, but they are now in 8-bit color depth. Director dithers to whatever bit depth and palette happens to be acting on the stage at the time bitmaps are imported.

5. The first step in working with the score of a new movie is to determine its stage size. From the cast window, drag the composite image of Organic's logo (the cast member named OrgComp.pic) to the upper left corner of the stage.

   OrgComp.pic is now a sprite in the score. It is the same size as in the cast. You can easily find out its exact size by choosing Score, Sprite Info. The width is 391 pixels and the height is 175 pixels; this is roughly the size we want to set the stage.

6. Set the stage size by choosing File, Preferences and entering a stage width of 384 and height of 171.

7. Click on the OrgComp.pic sprite in the stage and position it so that it is centered on the stage. You can use the cursor keys to move it one pixel at a time.

8. Another basic parameter to set is the tempo. This governs the maximum rate of playback.

   Double-click on the tempo channel of frame 1 and set the tempo slider to 15 frames per second. This caps off the rate of playback. Slower machines might not sustain this rate, but at least faster machines will not exceed it.

The next step is to slice up the bitmapped text *Organic ONLINE*.

9. In the cast window, click on the cast member Org1-bit.pic. Duplicate it by choosing Cast, Duplicate Cast.

10. Repeat this duplication 12 more times until you have one copy for each of the letters in the phrase *Organic ONLINE*.

11. Open the first copy of cast member Org1-bit.pic in the paint window by double-clicking on it in the cast window. This bitmap will be cut down until just the leafy *O* remains.

12. Remove everything but the leafy *O* using the rectangle marquee tool to select unwanted pixels. Then press the delete key to clear the unwanted selection within the rectangular marquee. Do this as many times as needed to reduce the image to the desired portion.

13. Repeat this deleting process with each of the 12 remaining copies of cast member Org1-bit.pic until each of the letters *r-g-a-n-i-c-O-N-L-I-N-E* exists as its own separate cast member.

14. In the paint window, you can automatically center the registration mark by double-clicking on the registration tool. Do this for each of the separate bitmapped letters in the cast.

Note

As a general rule, you should center the registration mark of your bitmap castmembers. The reason may not seem obvious. As you know, Director refers to the registration marks of the castmembers when displaying them as sprites on the stage. Shifting the registration mark of a given castmember will shift the stage position of all its sprite instances. When you import bitmaps, or paste into a bitmap, Director automatically centers the registration mark.

Building a score from cast members that have odd registration marks makes it potentially more cumbersome to edit the movie. For example, if a sprite is based on an oddly registered cast member, then changing the cast of that sprite to a centered cast could force you to waste time repositioning the sprite on the stage. Unless there is a specific reason not to do so, we recommend centered registration marks for easier editing later.

The first step of actually animating the logo is to lay the cast onto the stage, exactly re-creating the image of the original composite logo. You have already imported the original composite and placed it centered on the stage. This will be used for visual comparison when you lay out the separated cast members onto the stage. You then add the three lines and a circle to match these elements of the original logo.

15. Click on the score window to make it active. The composite logo OrgComp.pic is already in sprite channel 1, frame 1 in the score.

16. Click on the score cell at sprite channel 1, frame 1 and, keeping the mouse button down, drag to the right one frame. Sprite channel 1 should now be highlighted from frame 1 to 2.

17. Choose Score, In-Between Linear to extend the OrgComp.pic one frame in time.

18. Click on the empty cell in sprite channel 2, frame 1 to tell Director into which channel and frame to place the next sprite you drag onto the stage.

19. Click on the cast window to make it active.

20. Click on the leafy *O*. Drag it to the stage and position it over the correct spot on the composite background. Don't worry if it doesn't line up exactly to the reference right now.

21. Repeat this positioning step for each of the 12 remaining letters in the cast. As you drag each onto the stage, Director automatically places the sprites in the next available sprite channel of the current frame.

    The leafy *O* and the letters *r-g-a-n-i-c-O-N-L-I-N-E* are now roughly in their correct place on the stage.

You are now ready to add the three lines and a circle that make up the remaining elements in the static logo.

22. Choose Edit, Rewind to rewind to the first frame.

23. Choose Windows, Tools to open the tools window, and select the line tool. Select black in the foreground color chip. Select a 1-pixel line width (second from the top of the line choices).

24. One after another, draw three lines to match as closely as possible the stepped lines in the static logo.

25. Select the filled circle tool in the tools window. Draw a circle to match as closely as possible the punctuating circle on the right side of the long horizontal line in the static logo.

26. You can set the exact dimensions of the circle sprite. Select it and choose Score, Sprite Info, then set the height and width to 6.

You now fine-tune the position of the sprites:

27. Compare the position of the layered sprites in frame 1 to the reference image in frame 2. You can easily switch back and forth between the two frames using Command+right arrow and Command+left arrow in rapid succession (Control+left and Control+right in Windows).

28. One by one, adjust the shape and position of any misaligned sprites in frame 1 until there is little or no shift when you switch back and forth between frames 1 and 2.

The easiest way to tweak the position of sprites on the stage is to click on them either on the stage or in the score window, and then use the arrow keys to move them one pixel at a time in any direction.

When you are satisfied that the sprites are positioned exactly as in the composite reference, then you can swap in your background cast member OrgBG.pic to replace the composite logo sprite (OrgComp.pic) in channel 1, frame 1.

29. Click on the sprite in sprite channel 1, frame 1. This sprite is currently referenced to cast member OrgComp.pic. Click in the cast member OrgBG.pic in the cast window. Choose Score, Switch Cast Members to link the selected sprite to the selected cast member.

30. Comparing frame 1 and frame 2 as before, adjust the position of OrgBG.pic in sprite channel 1 of frame 1 until it is correct.

    Have you saved recently? If not, you should save now.

After doing much valuable work, you now have an image that looks just as it did hours ago. The only difference is that now all the graphical elements are independent objects in a Director cast ready to be animated.

Animating the Logo

Here you will learn more techniques for quickly animating your sprites in the score using in-betweening.

Now is a good time to reopen the finished version in Director (OrgWin.dir) and take another look at the animation. Examine the score. To make it easier to analyze the different parts of the animation in the score, we have color coded the frames (see fig. 7.2).

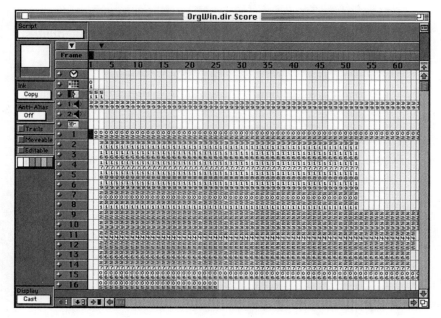

Figure 7.2

Color coding the score of the Organic Online Shockwave movie makes it easier to read and adds no file size after compressing with Afterburner.

Tip

Cell coloring can be switched on and off by choosing Score, Score Window Options and clicking in the Colored Cells check box.

After you have looked through the finished movie, open the current version you have been creating.

The first event in most Shockwave movies is the entrance. When the Organic Online movie starts, we want it to enter with a dissolve of the oval background and then a dissolve of the text and logo.

First, the stage color needs to match the background color that is used in its Web page.

1. Choose Window, Control Panel to open the control panel window, and use the color chip in the lower right corner to set the stage color. Select the gray color fifth from the right in the third row.

2. Now delay the entrance of the complete image by dragging and dropping the contents of frame 1 into frame 3.

3. In the score window, select all the sprites you put in frame 1 by click-dragging from sprite channel 1 down to the highest occupied channel. Let go of the mouse button now.

4. Position the cursor over the highlighted chunk of sprites; the arrow turns to a hand. Drag and drop the chunk to frame 3.

5. Click on the leftover reference sprite in channel 1, frame 2. Press delete to clear it.

6. Click on the sprite in channel 1, frame 3. Let go of the mouse button. While holding down the Option key (Alt in Windows), drag and drop the sprite one frame to the left. This duplicates the sprite into channel 1, frame 2.

Tip

Holding the Option key (Alt in Windows) while dragging and dropping copies the highlighted sprites into the destination zone.

You now have the first three frames forming the correct entrance sequence.

Add the Desired Transition Effects

1. Double-click in the transition channel of frame 1. Scroll down the Set Transitions scrollbar and select the transition dissolve pixels. Choose a 1 1/2-second duration (6 quarter seconds).

2. Tween this same transition into frame 2 and 3 by click-dragging on the transition channel from frame 1 to frame 3. Then choose Score, In-Between Linear.

Rewind and play the movie to check out your work. It should open with a blank gray screen, dissolve the oval background, dissolve the organic logo, and then loop back to the start.

Animating Frames 4–17

1. After the complete logo dissolves, it should sit for about a second to give the viewer time to read it. Choose Score, In-Between Linear to extend all sprites in time to frame 17.

2. Click and drag from sprite channel 1, frame 1 down and to the right to sprite channel 18, frame 17.

3. Choose Score, In-Between Linear to extend the sprites in time.

Animating Frames 18–22

Bring the stepped lines to life making them appear to be part of a single tensioned wire of some kind. The black circle on the right tip of the long horizontal line pulls to the right and the stepped lines on the left straighten to a single diagonal with the *O* of the word *ONLINE* acting as a pulley or fulcrum.

To achieve this effect use tweening.

Tip

A basic method of tweening is to set the starting and ending spatial positions of the sprites and then set their separation in time. These two frames are known as *keyframes.* Adjust the amount of frames separating the two keyframes before you tween. Just add or subtract frames in between by using the Score, Insert Frame or Score, Delete Frame command. Then select the region in the score that bridges the sprites of the keyframes. Issuing the Score, In-Between Linear command calculates intermediate positions for all the sprites and smooth motion in between the keyframes is achieved.

1. Create an ending keyframe by copying the sprites from frame 17 into frame 22. Click and drag from sprite channel 1 down to sprite channel 18, frame 17. Then, while holding the Option key (Alt in Windows), drag and drop a copy of the block into frame 22. Make sure the sprites are at the same level as the frame 17 sprites.

2. Now you arrange the sprites in the ending keyframe (frame 22) to appear as shown in figure 7.3. The long horizontal line with the circle at its right end is shifted right until its left tip lines up with the left edge of the *ONLINE* text. The length of each line does not change, nor does their linkage change.

Figure 7.3
Arrange the sprites in frame 22 to this appearance.

3. When you have them correctly oriented, you can tween them by clicking and dragging from sprite channel 1, frame 17 down and to the right to sprite channel 18, frame 22. Now choose Score, In-Between Linear to tween.

4. To simplify the next tweening, delete the redundant upper diagonal line. Click on the upper left of the two diagonal lines in frame 22. Notice where it intersects the leafy *O*. Press delete to clear it from the score.

5. Click on the lower diagonal and move its upper left handle to the spot on the leafy *O* previously intersected by the upper diagonal. It should appear as before, only the diagonal is now one line instead of two.

Animating Frames 22–27

The ending keyframe of the last operation becomes the new starting keyframe.

1. Select the sprites in frame 22 and copy them into frame 27 using Option+drag-and-drop (Alt+drag-and-drop in Windows).

2. Arrange the sprites in keyframe 27 to appear as in figure 7.4. The black circle has moved onto the very edge of the oval. The

horizontal line has grown to the right accordingly. The diagonal has shrunken down to a point and will disappear after this frame. It is still anchored to the same place on the horizontal line and to the leafy O, which is now colliding with the *ONLINE* text.

Figure 7.4
Arrange the sprites in keyframe 27 to this appearance.

3. When you have them all correctly oriented on the stage, select the sprite range from frame 22 to 27 and tween them by choosing Score, In-Between Linear.

4. Delete the last instance of the black circle sprite, which is in frame 27.

Animating Frames 27–32

The leafy O shrinks down until it is the same size and position as the letter O in *ONLINE*. The other letters of the word *Organic* are pulled toward *ONLINE* as if they are connected to the leafy O by some invisible elastic.

1. Select the sprites in frame 27 and copy them into frame 32 using Option+drag-and-drop (Alt+drag-and-drop in Windows).

2. Arrange the sprites in keyframe 32 to appear as shown in figure 7.5.

Figure 7.5
Arrangement of the sprites in keyframe 32.

3. When you have them all correctly oriented on the stage, select the sprite range from frame 27 to 32 and choose Score, In-Between Linear to tween them.

4. Go through each frame of the tween and tweak the position of the letters as needed.

Animating Frames 32–53

The rest of the word *Organic* is pulled down into the *O* in *ONLINE*. You will create five keyframes and tween them all at once.

1. Select the sprites in frame 32 and copy them into frame 37 using Option+drag-and-drop (Alt+drag-and-drop in Windows).

2. Arrange the sprites in keyframe 37 to appear as shown in figure 7.6.

3. Select the sprites in frame 37 and copy them into frame 42 using Option+drag-and-drop (Alt+drag-and-drop in Windows).

4. Arrange the sprites in keyframe 42 to appear as shown in figure 7.7.

Figure 7.6
Arrangement of the sprites in keyframe 37.

Figure 7.7
Arrangement of the sprites in keyframe 42.

5. Select the sprites in frame 42 and copy them into frame 46 using Option+drag-and-drop (Alt+drag-and-drop in Windows).

6. Arrange the sprites in keyframe 46 to appear as shown in figure 7.8.

Figure 7.8
Arrangement of the sprites in keyframe 46.

7. Select the sprites in frame 46 and copy them into frame 49 using Option+drag-and-drop (Alt+drag-and-drop in Windows).

8. Arrange the sprites in keyframe 49 to appear as shown in figure 7.9.

Figure 7.9
Arrangement of the sprites in keyframe 49.

9. Select the sprites in frame 49 and copy them into frame 53 using Option+drag-and-drop (Alt+drag-and-drop in Windows).

10. Arrange the sprites in keyframe 53 to appear as shown in figure 7.10. All the letters are now positioned over the letter O.

Figure 7.10
Arrangement of the sprites in keyframe 53.

11. Confirm that each of the keyframes has all its sprites correctly positioned on the stage, select the sprite range from frame 32 to 53, and choose Score, In-Between Linear to tween them.

12. Now go back through each frame of the tween and tweak the position of the letters as needed.

13. Finally, in frame 53, select the leafy *O* sprite and letter sprites of *r-g-a-n-i-c* and delete them from the score. Only the *ONLINE* and the horizontal line persists on the stage in frame 53.

Animating Frames 53–57

The word *ONLINE* gets condensed to the right like a spring being compressed by the pulling of the horizontal line.

1. Select the sprites in frame 53 and copy them into frame 57 using Option+drag-and-drop (Alt+drag-and-drop in Windows).

2. In keyframe 57, select the sprite with the letter *N* and move it horizontally to the right until it butts up against the *E*.

Tip

Repositioning sprites on the stage can by constrained to horizontal or vertical moves by holding the shift key as you drag.

3.   Then, butt the *I* to the *N*, the *L* to the *I*, and so on until the whole word is compressed to the right against the *E*.

4.   Move the left tip of the horizontal line under the right edge of the letter *O*.

5.   Select the sprite range from frame 53 to 57 and choose Score, In-Between Linear to tween them.

Animating Frames 57–66

The word *ONLINE* flies off and disappears to the right of the oval.

1.   Select the sprites in frame 57 and copy them into frame 66 using Option+drag-and-drop (Alt+drag-and-drop in Windows).

2.   In keyframe 66, select all sprites comprising the word *ONLINE*.

3.   Hold the shift key as you click on the letter *O* and drag to the right until the right edge of the *O* is just touching the right edge of the oval. The whole word *ONLINE* has moved off the oval.

4.   Click on the left tip of the horizontal line. Move it right until it is under the right edge of the letter *O*.

5.   Select the sprite range from frame 57 to 66 and choose Score, In-Between Linear to tween them.

6.   Go through each of the frames 57–66 deleting any letter sprites that slip off the right edge of the oval. There should be no encroaching on the gray background region. When you are done, frame 66 should show only the oval background.

If you haven't saved recently, save your work now. Rewind and play the movie to review your work. All the motion should be smooth and continuous, giving the sensation that all the elements are physically linked. If you are satisfied with your results, then proceed to the final animation steps.

Adding a Film Loop and a Sound Loop

You have just re-created most of the animation for the Organic Online shocked logo. Take a moment to study what you have done. The animation is harmonious and meaningful. The logo appears, and is read by the viewer. Then, following the natural reading rhythm, the logo consumes itself and pulls itself off the edge of its own environment. The motion implies connection and propagation. It feels as though the lines and letters have a physical link. Like a tensioned wire, the force of the line pulls everything through the gateway of the *ONLINE* text. It is a very stimulating and engaging animation, yet it has very simple and elemental properties.

Now all that is needed is a clever way to lead the logo back onto the stage so that it can be read over and over. When designing this originally, we tried several variations, such as dissolving it back in, flying it in from the other side, dropping it from the top, and so on. We finally arrived at the idea of letting the leafy *O* rotate and roll in from the right side back to its initial resting place. This works well because it brings the logo to life with the interesting behavior of falling and rolling. And, most important, it leads the eyes of the reader to the precise place where they will start to read the logo all over again.

Here you will be creating a film loop of the leafy *O* rotating. You will use the paint window to create multiple rotations of the leafy *O*. You will rotate the leafy *O* in increments of 45 degrees, creating a total of eight cast members for the film loop.

1. Before you begin creating the film loop, extend the background sprite to the 99th frame by selecting from the last occupied frame of sprite channel 1 out to frame 99 and choosing Score, In-Between Linear.

2. Now begin making the film loop. In the cast window, double-click on the leafy *O* cast member. This opens it in the paint window.

3. Duplicate this cast member by choosing Cast, Duplicate Cast Member.

4. Select the bounding box around the image by double-clicking on the rectangle marquee tool. This activates the Effects menu.

5. From the Effects menu, choose Free Rotate. Four handles appear in the corners of the marquee, and the cursor changes to crosshairs.

6. Click in the upper left handle and rotate the image clockwise until it is in the 315-degree position. Don't let go of the mouse button until you have made the exact rotation as shown in figure 7.11. This is a bit tricky. When it is rotated correctly, let go of the mouse button. Click off in an empty area of the paint window to perform the Free Rotate effect.

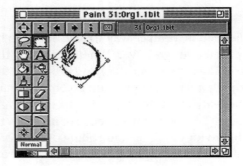

Figure 7.11
Use the Free Rotate effect to rotate the leafy *O* into this position.

7. Next, choose Effects, Auto Distort. Create seven new cast members. Choose OK and Director creates new cast members with the leafy *O* rotated to 45, 90, 135, 180, 225, 270, and 315 degrees.

Now it is time to turn these cast members into a film loop.

1. In the score window, click into sprite channel 2, frame 67.

2. In the cast window, make sure that the eight leafy *O* rotations are all next to each other in a row and in the correct order. Click on the first and then shift-click the last to select the whole range.

3. Choose Cast, Cast to Time. Select 1 frame apart. Notice that the eight cast members are laid out in the score in the same sequence as they appeared in the cast.

Because the leafy *O* is not a perfect circle, the registration mark does not perfectly correspond to the axis of rotation. Therefore, the rotation appears a bit jumpy.

4. Use Command+left-arrow and Command+right-arrow (Control+left and Control+right in Windows) to shuffle through the frames of the rotation sequence.

5. Fine-tune the position of each of the rotated sprites so that the motion is as smooth as possible. Make sure the ink is Background Transparent on all the sprites.

6. When this is complete, click and drag in sprite channel 2 from frame 67 to 75 in the score to highlight all eight sprites of the rotation sequence. Let go of the mouse button. Now drag and drop the selected block into the cast window. This creates a film loop out of the score selection.

Give the film loop an appropriate name.

Note that when you create a film loop Director encapsulates all the sprite information, including ink effects. Film loops on the stage refer to the ink effects as originally set in the score; therefore, applying ink to a film loop sprite has no effect.

Note

Next, you will lay this out on the score to simulate the motion of a rolling object falling down and up the basin of the background oval.

1. Clear sprite channel 2, frame 67–75 in the score.

2. Click in sprite channel 2, frame 67.

3. Drag the film loop from the cast window to a vertically centered position at the far right of the oval on the stage.

4. Activate the score window, then copy the film loop sprite in frame 67 by selecting Edit, Copy Cells. Paste 10 copies into sprite channels 3 through 12 of frame 67. Your score should now look roughly like figure 7.12.

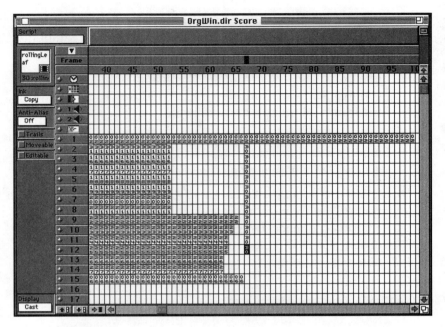

Figure 7.12
Arrangement of the score in frame 67.

You are using a new method of animation called *space-to-time animation.* Think of it as a long-exposure photograph of your animation. All the motion is condensed into one instant of time. You give the sprites the correct spatial arrangement and then use the Score, Space to Time command to sequence them at equal time intervals.

5. Lay out all the sprites in frame 67 so that they look like figure 7.13. It is important that the sprites be in the proper order in the sprite channels, so figure 7.12 shows which channel number corresponds to each sprite. Start by positioning sprite 12 to the proper location on the stage. Then position sprite 11 and 10 and so on.

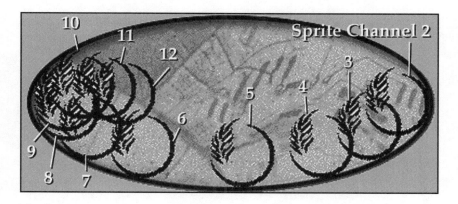

Figure 7.13

Arrangement of the stage in frame 67 before using the Space to Time command.

6. When you have arranged all the sprites correctly, highlight them all and choose Score, Space to Time. Spread the sprites three frames apart.

   They are now all in a sequence in time, each three frames apart.

7. With the sprites still highlighted, choose Score, In-Between Special.

8. Check the box next to In-Between: Location. Pull the path slider all the way to the right to apply an outside curve on the path. Specify a zero acceleration and deceleration, and choose OK.

Finalize the movie by looping the end back to the beginning position.

1. Click into the cell at sprite channel 2, frame 3. This is the first leafy *O* cast. Choose Edit, Copy Cells to copy the sprite.

2. Click into sprite channel 2 at frame 99 and paste (Edit, Paste Cells).

3. Click and drag in channel 2 from frame 97 to 99. Choose In-Between Linear.

4. Put a score script in frame 99 by double-clicking in the script channel of frame 99.

5. Type the following script:

```
on exitFrame
  go marker (-1)
end exitFrame
```

Press Enter.

6. Drag a marker onto the marker channel of frame 3.

The animation is now done. If you haven't saved recently, save your work now. Rewind and play the movie to review your work. Clean up any glitches you see. With the animation complete, the only thing left is to add sound.

The sound loop you will use was taken from a composition by Rocky Mullin, a production manager with Organic Online. He chose a part of his song suitable for looping and then looped it in SoundEdit16.

1. Choose File, Import and import the sound file WBLcrop.aif from the CD-ROM Ch07 folder.

2. In the cast window, double-click on the sound cast named WBLcrop.aif to get cast info.

3. Select the option for looped sound and choose OK.

4. Drag the WBLcrop.aif sound cast from the cast window to sound channel 1, frame 1.

5. Double-click on the sound channel 1 icon to the left of frame 1. This highlights sound channel 1 through the end of the movie.

6. Extend the sound by tweening (Score, In-Between Linear).

Rewind and play the movie to check out your work. If you are happy and there is no more cleanup to be done, you can perform the final step in shocking this logo.

Reducing the File Size of the Movie

Reducing the file size has been a design consideration at every step of this shockwaving process. Now that the movie is completed, you'll want to achieve the most file shrinkage possible. You can use the following basic checklist to determine if your finished movie is as small as possible:

- ⚡ Remove all unused cast members from the cast.

- ⚡ Only use very short sound loops sampled at 8 bits, 11.025 KHz.

- ⚡ Reduce the bit depth of bitmapped cast members as far as possible.

- ⚡ Use QuickDraw objects for all lines, circles, rectangles, and textures.

- ⚡ Use QuickDraw text wherever possible (very standard fonts only).

- ⚡ Reduce any textured bitmaps to its smallest grid size. Repeat this smaller cast on the stage to yield the original texture.

- ⚡ Use ink and color effects and scaling instead of adding cast members.

First, you'll want to remove all unused cast members. Since you know your movie intimately by now, you could do this by hand. But Director has a helpful resource to automatically select the unused cast members. This technique comes in handy for larger movies.

1. Choose Cast, Find Cast Members to display the Find Cast Members dialog box. Specify the option "Find cast members that are not used in the score" and choose Select All.

2. After inspecting each of the selected cast to make sure you don't really need them in the movie, choose Edit, Clear Cast.

3. After clearing the unused cast members choose File, Save As and save with a new filename. Whenever making major changes to the cast, you should save it as a new version immediately so that you can recover from unfortunate mistakes.

Warning

The procedure "Find cast members that are not used in the score" makes selecting and removing unused cast members a breeze. Beware though—it can have unintended results. Thankfully, using "Find cast members that are not used in the score" does not select movie scripts, cast scripts, or any cast members that are referenced by film loops that appear in the score. So, the main caveat to keep in mind is not to blow away cast members that are puppeted by your Lingo scripts and therefore might not appear in the score. Bitmaps, sounds, digital video, and text lists all can be referenced by Lingo scripts and therefore are potential victims of overzealous cast clearing. Think before you clear and keep backups.

4. Next, reduce the bit depth of all the unicolored cast members to 1-bit. Your bitmapped text is in this category, as well as the line-art leafy *O* logo.

5. In the cast window, select all the cast members to be reduced to 1-bit. This includes all the letters of the text, the leafy *O,* and all the leafy *O* rotations used in the film loop.

Tip

Clicking on a cast member and then shift-clicking on another cast member highlights all cast members in between. You can also select and deselect cast members individually without disturbing the rest of the selection by holding the Command key (Control in Windows) and clicking or holding the Command key (Control in Windows) and shift-clicking. This is very helpful for selecting multiple cast members in a discontinuous range.

6. Choose Cast, Transform Bitmap.

7. Make sure the scale option is at 100 percent.

8. Select Color Depth: 1-bit, Palette: System-Win, and Remap to Closest Colors.

9. Choose OK and then OK after the dire warning of irreversibility.

10. Save As a new filename.

You have used two very important methods for reducing Shockwave files in size. You discarded the unused cast and reduced the bit depth as much as possible. You can still do some minor tweaking to squeeze it down a bit more, but the only way to get significant shrinkage now is to redesign the animation, use smaller and fewer cast members, and/or use a shorter sound loop.

The Organic logo movie is now complete.

The finished movie is now ready to compress using Afterburner. If you followed along with the tutorial, the final movie should be less than 120 KB and less than 60 KB when burned. Congratulations. You did it.

You now need to embed the movie in the html page.

1. Drag the movie onto Afterburner. Save it as OrgWin.dcr in the Ch07/Movies folder.

2. Open the ex7_1.htm file in your text editor (it is in the Ch07 folder). At the bottom of the file, just before the **</body>** tag, add the lines:

    ```
    <center>
    <embed src="Movies/OrgWin.dcr" height=169 width=384>
    </center>
    ```

    Save the file and quit your text editor. Open the file in your browser.

EXAMPLE 7-2:

Shocking the Acclaim Technologies Logo

Now that you've shocked one logo, the only question remaining in your mind, no doubt, is "Which logo will I shock next?" In this section you will use the example of Acclaim Technologies' logo to learn more advanced techniques. You will not repeat the basic production steps you have been through in shocking Organic Online.

The basic approach to shocking a logo is now a given. With the Acclaim logo, you take on the specific design challenge of frame by frame, also known as *cell animation*. This adds an important skill to your repertoire.

Cell animation is a qualitative leap over the basic animation techniques that merely utilize sprite displacement, scaling, and rotation. With it you can take your Shockwave movies to a higher level of complexity and interest.

Painting a Frame-By-Frame Animation

Shocking logos can be a very creative experience that sometimes leads to designs that neither the artist nor the client expected. Often no design is specified at the outset of the production; the shock artist is simply asked to "work your magic." When Acclaim Technologies wanted their logo shocked, they gave us an EPS file of their static logo: an @ symbol casting a shadow, as shown in figure 7.14. The creative direction they wanted was to do something festive with some dancy bassy music.

Figure 7.14
The static Acclaim Technologies logo, waiting to be shocked.

Given that a rhythmic feel was requested, we decided to make the @ symbol dance to the beat, literally. The image of the @ is already suggestive of a spring, with potential motion waiting to uncoil. It has a sort of nervous energy, which we used in the character animation.

The second element in the static logo is the shadow of the @, which implies that lighting sources should play an important role in setting the environment of the shocked logo. The idea of having strobing or flashing lights as in a discotheque was a natural fit with the rest of the design.

To see the final shock logo design we developed, open and play the movie acclaim.dir in Director from the Ch07/Acclaim folder.

Note

Simply moving or rolling the @ logo around would not have given it enough personality. Frame-by-frame animation was necessary to give the @ logo any sort of interesting behavior. Morphing the @ into a pair of dancing arms gives the feeling there is something alive and expressive living inside, always moving or ready to move.

Frame-by-frame animation has a venerable tradition. It is sometimes called *cell animation,* referring to the transparent acetate cells on which the frames of handmade animations are painted. Hand animators stack their transparent cells as they paint so that they can reference their work to the previous or subsequent frames of the animation.

The hand animator's technique can be simulated using Photoshop (see the following Note). For cell animation, we prefer to use the program Fractal Design Painter for two reasons. Painter has a convenient multicell file format. You can create Painter files with multiple cells of bitmap images. The playback feature enables you to conveniently preview your animation sequence. And when you are done, each cell is separately saved as a numbered PICT file for fast importing into Director.

Using Photoshop for cell animation is a bit cumbersome, but it can be done. First, you must create a unique layer for each cell in the animation. Make a new file and set the mode to grayscale. Then open the Layers palette and from its pop-up menu, select New Layer. Make a layer for each of the cells in the movie.

Note

As you paint in a particular layer, you can display a useful overlay of the adjacent layer or layers for reference as you paint. All the settings needed to do this are found in the Layers palette. You choose which layer to paint in by clicking on its name. Make layers visible and invisible by clicking on the eyeball icon at the left of the layer names. The opacity of the active layer is set on the opacity slider.

When you are finished, you must make a new PICT file for each cell. Then you can cut and paste the contents of each layer, or you can drag and drop each layer from the Layer palette to the canvas of the empty new files. The untitled files must have the image flattened before you save as PICT. Make sure to name the PICT files in a correctly numbered sequence. These can then be imported into Director.

Cell animation is facilitated in Painter with the Tracing Paper feature. Using Tracing Paper enables you to see an overlay of two or more cells at once as you paint onto any one of them, simulating the traditional cell animation technique.

 Shortcut

You can skip this section and just use the Acclaim.ptr file from the CD-ROM Ch07/Acclaim folder.

1. Open Fractal Design Painter (version 3.0 or greater).

2. Open the file acclogo.pic from the Ch07/Acclaim folder of the CD-ROM.

3. Choose Edit, Select All and then Edit, Copy.

4. Make a new file (Command+N). Set the size to width: 320 pixels, height: 150 pixels, and 72 DPI. Choose Type, Movie with 17 frames. Make sure the paper color is white.

5. Press Return and then tell Painter where to save it and how to name it.

6. Painter now asks you to set tracing paper and bit depth options. Select 2 layers of Onion Skin and Storage Type: 8-bit grayscale.

7. Painter then takes a second to save off the 17 empty frames of your new multiframe animation.

First, notice the Frame Stacks window, shown in figure 7.15. It tells you which frames are in the onion skin stack and which is currently being edited. It has control buttons for going to the first and last frames and for flipping to the next or previous frame. It has stop and play buttons to project the cells in rapid succession, giving a preview of the animation.

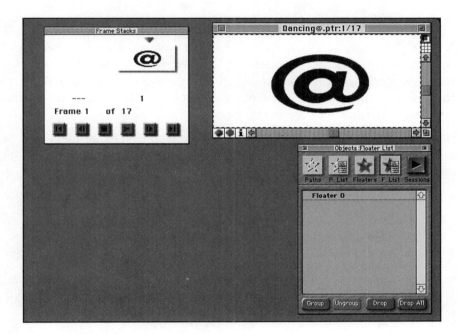

Figure 7.15

Pasting the Acclaim logo into the Canvas window at the first cell of our Painter movie. The Frame Stacks and Objects windows are shown.

8. You are in the first frame, frame 1 of 17. Choose Edit, Paste and paste the @ graphic.

    The @ graphic is now a floating image, or "floater 1" as it appears in the Object window's Floater List (F-list). Open the Object window by selecting Window, Object. (The Object window is also shown in figure 7.15.)

9 You must drop the floater either by clicking on the Drop button in the Object F-List window or choosing Edit, Drop. This commits the floating image to the canvas.

Frame 1 now has the @ logo in it.

10. Go to frame 2 by clicking on the next button in the Frame Stacks Window.

Now the fun really begins. A good part of the creative process in Painter is trying out different tools and modifying their settings until you can make the markings you want. We will tell you the exact settings of the tools we used in Painter to draw our animation, but this is not enough to enable you to draw it for yourself.

Here we present the basic drill that will get you started experimenting and practicing. If you have fun and have patience, you undoubtedly will come up with a really cool animation.

11. Make sure that the brush tool is active in the Tools window (Window, Tools).

12. Do some experimenting with different painting tools. Select one of the brushes in the Brushes window (Window, Brushes).

Remember, these cells will be reduced to 1-bit in Director. You want to use a brush that paints a solid and even-textured color. Try out felt pens, charcoal, and chalk.

13. Select the color black in the Art Materials: Colors window (Windows, Art Materials).

14. Start painting. Several parameters determine the shape and dynamics of the brush stroke.

Try changing the size and shape of the brush using the Brush Controls: Size window (Windows, Brush Controls). Pay particular attention to the parameters Size, ±Size, Squeeze, and Angle.

Brush dynamics such as size, angle, and opacity can be linked to mouse direction or velocity, your pressure tablet, randomness, and so on.

15. Using a pressure tablet with Fractal Design Painter is highly recommended. If you have tried this already, you know what

we mean. With a tablet, you can gain direct expressive control in Painter that is otherwise impossible to achieve.

Try linking the brush size to the tablet pressure using the Advanced Controls: Sliders (Window, Advanced Controls). See figure 7.16 to see how to slide the Size slider up to pressure. The size of the brush is now controlled by the pressure applied to the tablet. The minimum and maximum size is set using the ±Size setting in the Brush Controls: Size window (Window, Brush Controls). A larger ±Size setting exaggerates the effect of any size controller.

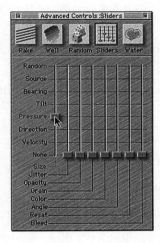

Figure 7.16

Use sliders in the Advanced Controls window to link various input to brush parameters.

If you only have a mouse as an input device, don't despair. You can still control brush size, angle, and so on with your mouse speed and direction. Just try linking different brush parameters to the velocity or direction of the mouse using the Advanced Controls: Sliders window.

16. Trying different preprogrammed brush types using the Brushes Window (Command+2) enables you to draw with different types of marks. Pay close attention to how the settings and behavior change as you experiment with new

brushes. Feel free to change any of the settings, and note the results. You can always restore the default settings of preprogrammed brushes.

17. Save your customized brush variations by choosing Tools, Brushes, Save Variant. Your variant as you named it will appear on the list of variants in the Brushes window.

Now that you've played around with different brushes and settings, take a look at the cells we created in the Acclaim shock logo animation. Open the file Acclaim.ptr from the Ch07/Acclaim folder. Choose 2 layers of onion skin. To preview this animation, press the play button in the Frame Stacks window.

We used a pressure tablet to create this cell animation. If you have a pressure tablet, choose the following settings:

- Brush window, Felt Pens: Felt Marker variation

- Brush Controls, Size window:

    Size = 13

    ±Size = 2.00

    Angle: Squeeze = 32%

    (Make sure to click on the Build button)

- Advanced Controls, Sliders window: Size slider on Pressure

- All other sliders on none

If you don't have a pressure tablet, you can get similar results with the mouse. Use the following settings:

- Brush Controls, Size window:

    Size = 21.3

    ±Size = 1.35

    Angle: Squeeze = 32%

    (Make sure to click on the Build button)

⚡ Advanced Controls, Sliders window: Size slider on Velocity

⚡ All other sliders on none

You are now ready to work on your cell animation. The first cell of your 17-cell file has the original Acclaim @ logo. By painting slight variations from one cell to the next, you can give the @ image any animated behavior you want.

1. Click on the next cell button in the Frame Stacks window. You should see a thumbnail of cell 1 and 2. The red carrot indicating which cell is currently being edited should be over cell 2. If it isn't, just click the thumbnail of cell 2 to move the red carrot over it.

2. Switch the Tracing Paper option on and off with Canvas, Tracing Paper, or click on the transparency button on the upper right of the canvas window. When transparency is on, frame 1 appears at 50 percent opacity as a visual reference. Painting black in the current frame also appears 50 percent gray. It shows 100 percent black only where the paint of the onion-skinned frames intersect.

3. Make a plan of attack for choreographing your animation, and then try to draw it cell by cell. You may have a different dance idea than ours, or another animation of the @ entirely. Let your imagination loose.

Tip

Making a bandwidth-efficient cell animation means not having redundant frames. Remember, once in Director, you can sequence the animation in forward and then reverse order to create a closed loop. In our Acclaim movie, we go forward through the whole dance and then again in reverse, the @ turning into a dancer and then back to an @ again. Then the @ twitches about for a while, alternating among the first three or four frames. You can get quite a variety of behaviors from 17 small 1-bit PICTs.

The approach we took was to have the @ unwind itself in the first few cells. By the seventh cell, the image fully resembles the two hands and arms of a dancer busting out into an exaggerated pose.

The hands are the most visually important component of the dancer. Smooth motion of shoulder and arm lines from pose to pose gives your figure personality. Do not attempt realism in the proportions or the profile of the lines. It is expressive and fluid. This is how you should feel when you paint. Imagine the sensation in the muscles of the arms and hands of the dancer, and let those sensations translate into your hand as you draw.

If you find yourself going down a blind alley with your animation, you can clear the unwanted contents of any frame. Just choose Edit, Select All and press the delete key. Also, you can insert or delete frames as needed with commands in the Movie menu.

If you haven't saved recently, now is a good time. After you have worked your animation for a while, press play in the Frame Stacks window to preview it.

4. When you are happy with your animation, choose File, Save As, with the save options set to Save movie as numbered files.

5. Choose PICT file type and name it something like accl001.pic. This creates a separate PICT with numbered names starting at 001 for each frame of your animation.

Bringing the Cell Animation into Director

Your animation is now ready to be imported into Director.

1. Open Director. Choose File, Preferences and set the stage size to width = 288 and height = 120.

2. Choose File, Import and import all the numbered PICTs of your cell animation.

3. To get a quick preview of how your animation will play as a loop, just select all the PICTs you just imported in the cast. Then choose Cast, Cast to Time.

4. Duplicate the sequence in the score. Hold down the Option key (Alt in Windows), and click and drag the block of cells 17 frames to the right.

5. Reverse the sequence of the copied cells by choosing Score, Reverse Sequence.

6. Now rewind and play to see your animation loop. Note that there are redundant cells in the middle and the end that you might want to remove.

7. If you are satisfied with how this looks, reduce the bit depth of your cast to 1-bit. Choose Cast, Transform Bitmap and specify 1-bit and System-Win, and check the radio button map to the closest color.

You can now articulate your animation in the score by varying the order of the sprites in your sequence, their location, scaling, ink, and color within each frame. You can make a film loop or loops to facilitate flying the whole animation around. You can even have multiple instances of the animation on the stage at once with almost no additional cost in bandwidth.

Congratulations! You have made your very own character animation using the cell animation method. You can reward yourself by remembering to save your file. Next, you will learn about animating with texture and color.

Tweening Color

You already have learned to tween the location and scaling of sprites. Now you will learn to tween color as well using the In-Between Special command. This enables you to quickly apply color animation to your sprites by cycling through adjacent colors in the palette.

A foreground and background color can be applied in the score to any 1-bit sprite or QuickDraw sprite (lines, circles, and so on). The foreground and background colors can be tweened independently. If the sprite's ink is set to background transparent, you cannot see the background color. Copy or Matte ink enables you to see the background color.

Note

QuickDraw text can also be given foreground and background color, but this changes the cast member itself, and thus all other sprite instances of it change too. So, to animate the color of QuickDraw text, you need a separate text cast member for each of the colors used in your animation. Or, use Lingo to set and reset the color of the text cast (see the following section, "Lingo Control of Color").

1. To apply color tweening to your Acclaim logo character animation, open the Director file that has your Acclaim logo animation as a sequence of 1-bit images in the score.

2. In the score, click on the first sprite of the animation.

3. In the tools window (choose Window, Tools), select any color. Your sprite should now change to that color. If it didn't, make sure the cast is 1-bit and the ink is Background Transparent.

4. Now, click on the middle sprite of the animation.

5. In the tools window, select a different color (far away from the first color you selected in the palette).

6. Now, highlight from the first sprite to the middle sprite in the score and choose Score, In-Between Special.

7. Check only the box for In-Between: foreground. Select zero acceleration and a linear path. Choose OK.

8. Then, in the same fashion, change the color of the last sprite so that it is the same as the color of the first sprite.

9. Highlight from the middle sprite to the last sprite and choose Score, In-Between Special.

10. Check only the box for In-Between: foreground. Select zero acceleration and a linear path. Choose OK.

When you play the movie, you will see the color of the sprite cycle through adjacent colors in the palette from your start color to your end color and then back again.

You can obtain gradual or radical color tweening depending on your choice of starting and ending colors. In the windows palette, contiguous color gradations exist for reds, blues, pinks, and greens. You can't use tweening to get smooth gradations for other colors, however; you have to apply colors individually to the sprites.

Advanced Animating with Color and Patterned Fills

In this section, you learn techniques of color, texture, and ink control that can add excitement and attention-getting power to your movies. Animating with color and patterned fills takes up little or no extra file size in your movie. This makes color and patterned fills an important part of your Shockwave bag of tricks.

Lingo Control of Color

An advanced technique in color animation is to use Lingo to set the foreground and background colors. For example, the following score script will assign a random foreground color to the sprite in channel 1:

```
on enterFrame
  puppetSprite 1, TRUE
  set x = random (255)
  set the foreColor of sprite 1 to x
  updateStage
end
```

The following score script assigns the color red to the text cast under the mouse cursor:

```
on enterFrame
  --This only works for text cast
  set x = the mouseCast
  if x > 0 then set the foreColor of cast x to 6
  --Red is 6 in the windows palette
  UpdateStage
end
```

The Lingo commands to use for setting and testing color follow:

- ⚡ foreColor of sprite (only for 1-bit and QuickDraw sprites)

- ⚡ backColor of sprite (only for 1-bit and QuickDraw sprites)

⚡ foreColor of cast (only for text cast)

⚡ backColor of cast (only for text cast)

Patterned Fills

Director has 64 different QuickDraw patterns that can be applied. Eight of these patterns are editable; the noneditable patterned fills are 1-bit textures. When applied to sprites, the foreground and background colors of the pattern can be independently assigned.

Note

Patterned fills have several limitations. Patterned fills can only be assigned to filled QuickDraw cast members such as ovals and rectangles. Patterns cannot be given to the sprites of 1-bit cast or text cast.

Pattern data is associated with the cast member and not with the sprites in the score. Changing the pattern of a QuickDraw sprite in the score changes the cast member and thus all other instances of it. So, you need a separate QuickDraw cast member for every distinct pattern you want to apply. This is not a big memory drain, just a minor nuisance.

Patterned fills cannot be tweened in the score or controlled by Lingo scripts. You have to assign patterns by hand in the score.

Now you practice modifying the colors and patterns of QuickDraw sprites using the Acclaim Shockwave movie as an example. Using colors and patterns lets you be generous with impact and thrifty with bandwidth.

1. Open the file acclaim.dir from the Ch07/Acclaim folder of the CD-ROM. Play the movie and notice how the interplay of color and texture in the background creates a pulsating, almost hypnotic environment for the Acclaim logo.

2. Use the Window, Tools and Window, Score commands to open the tool window and the score window.

3. Click on sprite 1 in frame 40. This is the QuickDraw rectangle that forms the background.

4. When you click on a patterned QuickDraw sprite, its pattern is shown in the pattern chip of the tools window.

5. Click on sprite 1 in the subsequent frames to see how each sprite has a different patterned fill and foreground/background color.

Try changing the patterns and colors of the sprites in the movie to see how this affects the feel of the movie. First, set a range of sprites to a particular color. Then, set smaller ranges to alternating colors, pulsating in time with the beat of the music. Or, see how it looks if you vary the colors and patterns from one frame to the next.

Advanced Ink Effects

Another bandwidth-savvy way to add a great deal of visual excitement to your movies is to use ink effects. When applied smartly, inks can create dynamic new shapes and moods with no cost to bandwidth. Ink effects in Director allow colors from two or more sprites to interfere with each other on the stage, creating new color output.

Ink effects in Director are conceptually similar to layer modes in Photoshop. All sprites are assigned an ink effect in the score. For each pixel of the sprite, Director calculates an output color. The three variables used in this ink rendering calculation are: 1 for the chosen ink of both sprites, 2 for the foreground pixel color, and 3 for the underlying pixel color.

Inks are a live-rendered effect. That is, ink effects rely on the processing power of the user's machine to render them to the stage as the movie plays. This affords a great savings in file size, at a cost of processing speed.

Some ink effects use complex calculations and are quite slow in rendering. As a general rule, inks that are lower on the pop-up list of ink effects in the score window are slower to render. Therefore, ink effects should be applied thoughtfully. Movies with intensive use of ink effects should be tested on machines running at your minimum hardware requirement to confirm performance.

Very interesting effects can be achieved when different combinations of ink effects are applied to identical copies of the same sprite. You should experiment with many permutations of sprite layering, ink, and color. We have included a small demo movie that shows several ink techniques ink.dir, which is discussed in the following section and found in the Ch07 folder.

Reverse Ink

In Director, open the movie ink.dir from the Ch07 folder. Playing the movie illustrates three uses of Reverse ink. When you are through playing the movie, open up the score window and examine how the ink effects were applied. To see the ink effects most clearly, set the score to show the ink information by choosing ink from the views pop-up in the lower left corner.

The movie has four parts. After the introductory screen, the simplest use of Reverse ink is shown (see fig. 7.17): a 1-bit bitmap of a circle has Reverse ink applied to it, and anything that it passes over has its color reversed. The output color does not depend on the color of the reversing sprite; it depends only on the colors in the underlying image.

Figure 7.17
A sprite with Reverse ink.

When a Reverse ink sprite covers another Reverse ink sprite, they cancel each other out and the image disappears at their intersection. The second Reverse ink example in the movie ink.dir shows this very useful technique (see fig. 7.18). This is a great way to liven up moving text or any solid shapes.

Figure 7.18
Double Reverse ink cancels out at the intersection.

In the final example, we form a Reverse-ink sandwich out of three sprite channels (see fig. 7.19). The three channels are assigned the inks Reverse-Background Transparent-Reverse. This technique enables you to fill the shape of a sprite with the image of another sprite.

Here is how it works. The two identically patterned QuickDraw sprites are given Reverse ink, and so they negate each other and become invisible. The 1-bit text image is sandwiched between them and has Background Transparent ink. The foreground sprite becomes visible wherever it covers the middle layer image.

Figure 7.19
Double Reverse ink is uncancelled by the sandwiched sprite.

With this technique you can fill a pattern into any 1-bit bitmap. There is no other way to do this. Filling text with a QuickDraw pattern or a 1-bit texture is a great way to give text some personality.

Lingo Ink Control

In addition to setting ink directly in the score, you can test and set the ink assigned to puppeted sprites by using Lingo. Use the Lingo command "ink of sprite." To see an example of Lingo control of sprite ink, see the movie script of the ink.dir movie.

The ink.dir movie has simple navigation buttons to move forward and back through the examples. When the mouse clicks over a button, the movie script puppets the button sprite and changes the ink from Matte to Reverse ink. It switches the ink back to Matte when the mouse slips off the button, and also when the mouse button goes up.

Many other effects can be achieved using inks. These are the best performers and the most commonly needed. Experimenting with ink effects in your movies is sure to result in more bang for your bandwidth.

In performing the excercises of this chapter, you have animated two corporate logos. Along the way you have learned to use Photoshop to decompose a composite image and then recompose the pieces in Director and animate them. You have done a simple cell animation in Fractal Design Painter and then learned to get a big punch out of it in Director without taking a bit hit in filesize. Finally, you learned to animate the elements of color and pattern and ink to astound your viewer without the delay of big downloads.

In chapter 9 you create movies that demonstrate more of Shockwave's navigational agility. You will create two diagrams: one will represent locations in a Web site, the other represents locations in a shopping mall. Both illustrate important applications of Shockwave as a navigation interface.

CHAPTER 8

Diagrams

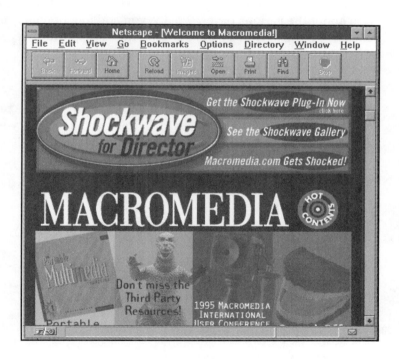

I n this chapter you explore some other uses for the rollover function in Lingo, as well as see how Shockwave can be used for active maps. You explore two examples of active diagrams: a map of a Web site and a fictional mall floor plan.

EXAMPLE 8-1:

Web Site Map

As well as new uses for rollovers, this example explores another vital tool in the Shockwave developer's toolbox: tiles. Tiles are repeated bitmaps or patterns, and are an excellent way to add visual interest to a movie at very little cost.

For this example you map the fictional Web site, then add active information about the various pages. Finally, you add functionality so that clicking on the icon of a page will send the user to the page.

Mapping the Site

For this exercise we used the same fictional site as for the control panel example (example 6-2 in chapter 6). In this case, however, you add some subpages to make the map more interesting, and to provide some information about the people in Squid Systems, Inc.

The structure of the site is outlined in figure 8.1.

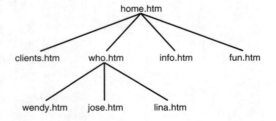

Figure 8.1
The map of the Squid Systems, Inc. Web site.

1. Open Director. Choose File, Preferences and set the stage size to 400×300.

2. Choose File, Movie Info. Set the default palette to System-Windows.

Import the file page.pic from the Ch08 folder, or execute the following five steps:

3. Open the paint window. Set the foreground color to black and the line width to 1.

4. Draw a rectangle approximately 25 pixels wide by 35 pixels high.

5. Draw a series of horizontal lines, approximately 3 pixels apart, stopping and starting almost at the edge of the rectangle. In the middle of the image, make one line end early and the following one start late. This is the basic page graphic, and should appear approximately as shown in figure 8.2, a.

Now you add an upturned corner.

6. Starting approximately 8 pixels in from the left edge of the rectangle, draw a 45-degree line from the top to the left edge of the rectangle. Erase everything outside that line.

7. Draw a vertical line down from the point at which the diagonal line meets the top edge to even with the point at which the diagonal meets the left edge. Draw a horizontal line from the left edge to intersect the vertical line at its end (see fig. 8.2, b).

a   b

Figure 8.2
The page graphic as it appears before (a) and after (b) adding an upturned corner.

8. Drag the page graphic onto the stage about one-third of the way down and centered.

9. Drag the graphic onto the stage again, roughly 50 pixels below the previous one and close to the left edge.

10. Drag three more copies onto the stage, distributed across the page equal with the second one.

11. Drag three more copies onto the stage underneath the second graphic in the second row. In the score, select all the sprites and specify Matte ink. Your stage should look like figure 8.3. Save the file as sitemap.dir in the Ch08 folder.

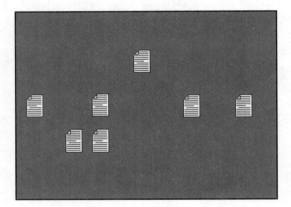

Figure 8.3
The page graphics are arranged on the stage following the logic of the site.

12. In the tool palette, set the foreground color to a dull yellow and draw lines connecting the top graphic to the four in the second row and the second graphic in the second row to the three below it (see fig. 8.4).

13. Open the paint window and set the foreground color to a bright yellow.

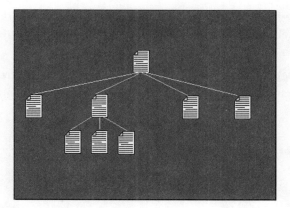

Figure 8.4
The lines show the links between pages.

14. Select the fancy font of your choice (this example uses Bodoni Poster) and set the size to 18 points. Type `Home`. Press the + key on the paint window toolbar to make a new cast member and type `Clients` in the same font. Repeat with `Who`, `Info`, and `Fun`. Change the size to 14 points and repeat with `Wendy`, `Jose`, and `Lina`.

15. Drag the cast members underneath their respective graphics (top to bottom, left to right, in order). Select all the text sprites and set their inks to Background Transparent.

You now add a title to the map.

16. Open a new paint cast member. Select the same font you used for the text sprites, but size it at 24 points this time. Set the foreground color to red. Type `Squid Systems, Inc.`, then click away from the text to commit it. Change the size to 18 points. Approximately 20 pixels underneath the first line, type `www.squidsys.com`. Move the second line so that it is centered under the first.

17. Click and hold the marquee tool until the pop-up appears. Select See Thru Lasso.

18. Select all the text. Option-drag (Alt-drag in Windows) the selection far enough away from the original so that they don't overlap.

19. Set the destination color chip (see fig. 8.5) to the same yellow used for the page names, then choose Effects, Switch Colors.

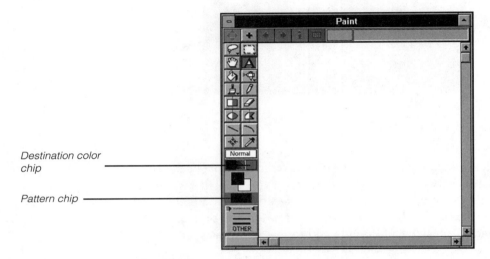

Destination color chip

Pattern chip

Figure 8.5

The destination color chip is used for switching colors and for gradients. The pattern chip, discussed later in this chapter, is used for adding tiles or patterns to an image.

20. Drag the now-yellow text on top of the red text, two pixels above and to the left of it.

21. Close the paint window. Drag the title cast member onto the stage, above the home page graphic, horizontally centered on the stage. Make sure the ink is set to Background Transparent. Save the file. The stage should now look like figure 8.6.

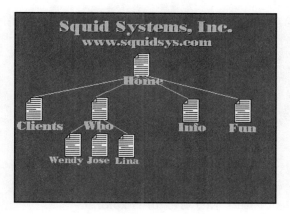

Figure 8.6

We add a title to the map so it is clear what we are charting, adding a second copy of the text to give a 3D effect.

Now you need a text box so that you can show some quick information about each page.

22. Select the text tool on the tool palette. Drag a text box underneath the third row of page graphics from approximately 20 pixels from the left edge of the stage to approximately 20 pixels from the right edge.

    FIELD

23. Control-click or press Command+I (right-click or Control+I in Windows) on the text sprite to bring up the Cast Info dialog box. In the name field, type **desc**. In the style pop-up, select fixed. Choose OK. The fixed style keeps the text box from resizing itself.

24. The text field on the stage now has a resize handle on its lower right corner. Drag this handle down to make about 10 pixels of space between the bottom of the text box and the bottom of the stage.

25. Click in the text box. Choose Text, Border, 2 pixels; then choose Text, Font, Times (Times New Roman in Windows).

    MODIFY— BORDER...

26. In the score, set the ink of the text sprite to Copy. Save the file.

The final step before adding functionality is to add a background. You can either create the background in Photoshop or use the following Shortcut to import the file from the *Macromedia Shockwave for Director User's Guide* CD-ROM.

Shortcut

Import file liltile.pic from the Ch08 folder if you want to skip the following 10 steps.

1. Open Photoshop. Select File, New and set the size to 200×200 pixels.

2. Select Filters, KPT, Texture Explorer.

3. Choose the Liquids, Midnight Blue Water preset.

4. Click and hold on the preview image until the pop-up appears.

5. Select Tile Size of 128×128. Choose OK.

6. Select a 64×64 pixel (exactly) square of the image.

7. Choose Filters, KPT, Seamless Welder.

8. Click on the warning box to dismiss it.

9. Choose Edit, Crop.

10. Choose File, Save and select PICT in the Type pop-up. Save the file as liltile.pic. Either 16 or 32 bits is OK. Quit Photoshop.

Switch to Director. Open sitemap.dir. Import the liltile.pic file.

1. In the score, select all the sprites and drag them one channel down in the score. They should now start at channel 2.

2. Open the liltile.pic cast member in the paint window by double-clicking on it.

3. Choose Paint, Tiles to display the Tiles dialog box.

4. Select the Created from Cast Member # radio button (see fig. 8.7). Click on the forward or backward arrow until the liltile.pic cast member appears in the left window.

5. Specify 64 in both the Width and Height pop-ups. You should see a seamless image in the right window. Choose OK.

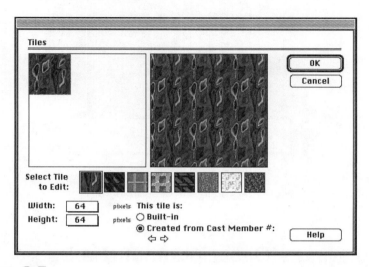

Figure 8.7

The Tiles dialog box allows you to use cast members as tiles.

Tiles are a good way to fill a large area with a texture without adding much download time. The limitations are that the tile size must be divisible by 16 pixels in both dimensions, and that you must fill a QuickDraw shape, not a paint object, to gain a file-size advantage.

Tip

6. Select the filled rectangle tool in the tool palette. Specify 0 line width and select the tile you've just created in the pattern pop-up (right below the color chips).

7. Drag out a rectangle that covers the entire stage. If it is not in channel 1 of the score, drag it there. Save the file.

Layout is done. Your stage should look like figure 8.8.

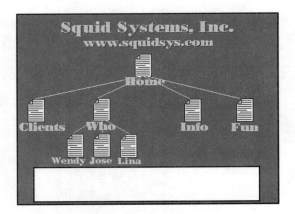

Figure 8.8
The final layout, with background and description box.

Displaying a Description of the Page

In this section you learn to display information about the page whose icon the mouse is over.

1. Choose an empty cast member and choose Window, Script to open a new Movie Script. Type the following script:

```
on checkFrame
  global gDescList
  repeat with i = 2 to 9
    if rollover(i) then
      put getAt(gDescList, i-1) into field "desc"
      exit
    end if
  end repeat
  put "" into field "desc"
end
```

This script checks each of the page icon sprites to see if the mouse is over it. If it is, the script finds the appropriate text item in the global description list and puts it into the description text box. If the mouse is not over a sprite, the script empties the description field. The reason we get item i-1 when the mouse is over sprite i is that the first page icon sprite is number 2, whereas the first item in the list is number 1.

2. In the same movie script cast member, type the following script:

```
on startMovie
  global  gDescList
  put "" into field "desc"
  set gDescList = ["home page", "Who are our clients?",¬
"Who we are", "Useful information about us, and other¬ things that may or
may not be important", "Fun Stuff",¬ "Wendy O is our resident technical
wizard and general¬ handywoman", "Jose R is the artist extraordinaire",¬
"Lina H can do anything, as long as you don't ask her ¬ to do it before
noon"]
end
```

The startMovie script is executed at the very beginning of a movie, before the movie actually draws the stage. This script identifies the variable gDescList as a global variable, so that it is accessible from other scripts (like the checkFrame script). It then clears the description field. Finally, it sets up the contents of the list so that the checkFrame script can grab them when needed.

3. In the score select all channels in frames 1 and 2. Choose Score, In-Between Linear.

4. Select the script channel in frame 2. Click on the script bar and type the following script, which loops the movie on the last frame, invoking the checkFrame handler each time:

```
on exitFrame
  checkFrame
  go the frame
end
```

Adding the GoToNetPage Functionality

You now need to add the code to make the movie go to the page whose
icon was clicked.

1. In the score, click on the Home page icon sprite (in channel 2).
   Select frames 1 and 2, channel 2. Click on the script bar and
   type the following script:

```
on mouseUp
  goToNetPage("../home.htm")
end
```

2. Select frames 1 and 2, channel 3 (the Clients page icon). Click
   on the script bar and type the following script:

```
on mouseUp
  goToNetPage("../clients.htm")
end
```

3. Repeat with each icon sprite. The page name is the icon title
   with ".htm" after it, but in all lowercase.

Save and run the file. You should get status messages every time the
mouse passes over a page icon.

Embedding the File in the HTML Page

Open the info.htm file in your text editor. Underneath the **<h2>** line, add
the lines:

```
<center>
<embed src="Movies/sitemap.dcr" width=400 height=300>
</center>
```

Save the file and open it in your browser. Clicking on the icon should go
to the appropriate page.

In the next example you add more extensive rollover information to a
mall map diagram.

EXAMPLE 8-2:

Mall Map Diagram

In this example you use the rollover function to highlight the area the mouse is over and also display information. You could easily have the sprites be clickable as well, but for the purposes of this exercise, we assume that we have covered that sufficiently already. We use a map of an imaginary mall to demonstrate the flexibility of the rollover function. This map could easily be an office floor plan, a zoning map, or many other possibilities.

You import a floor plan created in CorelDRAW!, add information about each store, and make the movie display the name and phone number of the store as well as additional information.

Laying Out the Mall Map

1. Open Director. Choose File, Preferences and set the stage size to 240×344 pixels.

2. Select File, Movie Info and set the default palette to System-Windows.

3. Set the stage color to blue.

4. Import the mall1.pic file from the Ch08 folder on the CD-ROM. Drag the cast member onto the stage approximately 30 pixels from the top, centered horizontally.

5. From the Ink pop-up menu, apply Matte ink to the sprite.

Now that you have the basic map, you need to add text boxes to display the store name, a short description, and the phone number.

6. In the tool palette, set the foreground color to black and the background color to 50 percent gray. Using the text tool, drag a text box in the lower left half, from 4 pixels from the left edge to 4 pixels from the white area of the map. With the text cast member selected in the cast window, Choose Cast, Cast Member Info, name the cast member `name`, and set the type to

fixed. Extend the cast member vertically until it is approximately three times as tall as it was originally, as shown in figure 8.9. Select the text sprites in the score and set the ink to Copy.

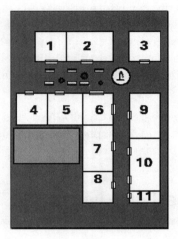

Figure 8.9
The "name" field will display the name of the store.

7. Click in the text field and specify the 12-point Times font with bold applied and a 2-pixel border.

8. Drag another field directly below and the same width as the first, select it in the cast window, and choose Cast, Cast Member Info. Name the cast member **desc** and set the type to fixed. Extend it vertically to about 20 pixels from the bottom of the stage.

9. Click in the text field and specify the Times font, 12-point, normal, with a 2-pixel border.

10. Drag a third text field, underneath and the same width as the second. Control-click (right-click in Windows) on the sprite to bring up the Cast Info dialog box and name the field **phone**.

11. Click in the text field and specify the same 12-point Times font with a 2-pixel border.

12. In the paint window, set the foreground color to dark blue and type `Squidville Mall` in the 18-point fancy font of your choice. Place at the top of the stage, making sure the ink effect is set to Background Transparent. Save the file in the Ch08 folder as mall.dir. Your stage should now look something like figure 8.10.

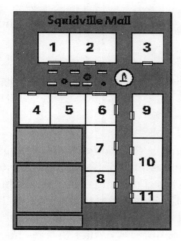

Figure 8.10

The final layout of the mall map contains three text fields—for names, descriptions, and phone numbers of the imaginary stores.

Marking the Map

You now need to mark the area covered by each store so that users will know when the mouse is over it. You also need to make a red rectangle to mark the store the mouse is over.

1. Select the unfilled rectangle tool. Set the line width to 0.

2. Click on frame 1, channel 7 of the score. On the stage, draw a rectangle with the same dimensions as store 1.

3. Draw, in order, a rectangle on each store on the map. The rectangles should fill channels 7–17.

4. Click on channel 47.

5. In the tool palette, set the foreground color to red and the line width to 2.

6. Draw a moderately sized (less than 100 pixels square) rectangle anywhere on the stage.

7. Choose Score, Sprite Info and set the distance from left edge of stage to −100.

8. Select frames 1 and 2, channels 1–17. Choose Score, In-Between Linear.

The layout of the movie is now complete. Save the file.

Adding Action

Now add the Lingo to make the movie do two things when the mouse is over a store: display some information about the store, and highlight the store on the map with a red rectangle. If we were more ambitious, it would be easy to add the capability to click on each store and go to another page, but that topic has been covered extensively in previous examples, including example 8-1 earlier in this chapter.

1. Select the script channel in frame 1. Click on the script bar. Type the following script:

```
on exitFrame
  puppetSprite 47, TRUE
end
```

2. Select the script channel in frame 2. Click on the script bar. Type the following script:

```
on exitFrame
  checkframe
  go the frame
end
```

3. Select an empty cast member and choose Window, Script to open a new script window. Type the following script:

```
on checkframe
  global gNameList, gDescList, gPhoneList
  repeat with i = 7 to 17
    if rollover(i) then
      set the rect of sprite 47 to the rect of sprite i
      put getAt(gNameList, i-6) into field "name"
      put getAt(gDescList, i-6) into field "desc"
      put getAt(gPhoneList, i-6) into field "phone"
      exit
    end if
  end repeat
  set the loch of sprite i to -100
end
```

This script tests each of the invisible rectangles. If it finds one of them has the mouse over it, the script displays the name, description, and phone number of each store in the corresponding text field by selecting the appropriate entry in the various lists, which are initialized in the following script. It also sets the bounding rectangle of the marker sprite to the same as the invisible rectangle. If the mouse is not over any store, the script moves the marker rectangle off the stage.

4. In the same movie script cast member, type the following script:

```
on startMovie
  global gDescList, gPhoneList, gNameList
  put " " into field "name"
  put " " into field "phone"
  put " " into field "desc"
  set gDescList=["Authorized Nikon and Minolta dealers","Specializing in
Contract and Tort Law",¬
"Fashion eyewear for the whole family","Prime retail space available. Call
the phone number below",¬
"Specializing in commercial property","Something special for him or her",¬
"Everything you expect from a mall record store","The business of
Squidville is business",¬
"Freshest Seafood in town","We have all the best sellers","We put the E in
Shoppe"]
```

```
  set gNameList =["Vlad's Camera Shop", "Ramirez, Chen and Hassad,
Attorneys at Law",¬
  "Smith and Sons Eyewear", "Available", "Baikunin Realty","Leon's
Lingerie","Really Expensive Records",¬
"Squidville Chamber of Commerce", "Uncle Joe's House of Seafood", "Mall
Books",
  "Phil's Smoke Shoppe"]
  set gPhoneList = ["(510) 553-4242","(510) 222-5147","(510) 488-
9008","(510) 332-0759", "(510) 332-0759",¬
"(510) 354-8000","(510) 897-2190","(510) 332-6145","(510) 979-9000","(510)
667-7233","(510) 357-7000"]
end
```

This script does nothing but clear the text fields at the beginning of the movie, then initializes the three lists.

5. Save the movie, then run it. Pass the mouse over the stores to make sure everything is correct.

6. Drag the movie onto Afterburner and save it as mall.dcr in the Ch08/Movies folder.

7. Open the ex8_2.htm file and add the following line:

```
<embed src="Movies/mall.dcr" height=344 width=240>
```

Open the file in your browser and test it. You should get status information each time you pass over a store on the map.

In this chapter you have seen some examples of using the rollover function to add realtime feedback. In the next chapter you return to the question of big graphic introductions.

CHAPTER 9

Advanced Rollover
Buttons

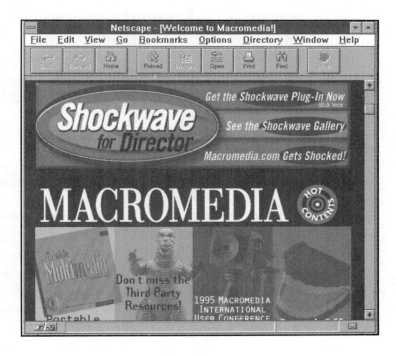

I n previous chapters you created Shockwave movies that used simple buttons to provide visual feedback when the mouse passes over them. This type of button is called a *rollover button*. The rollover function in Lingo was used to script these previous rollover button examples.

This chapter highlights a different and more sophisticated method for rollover button scripting. Here you will learn to use the mouseCast function in Lingo to script the behavior of rollover buttons. Doing the examples in this chapter will give you the ability to script movies with large numbers of buttons active at once, and movies with buttons that have nonrectangular hot spots.

Previewing the Sample Movies

Preparation: Copy the files from the CD-ROM Ch09 folder to your hard drive.

The first of the two movie examples in this chapter is Apple Computer's home page movie, affectionately called the "Gameboy" movie. With Apple's "Gameboy" movie, you will script the rollover behavior of the rollover buttons using the mouseCast function, and you will also learn how to script for dissimilar button behaviors.

Open the Director application, then open the movie apple.dir from the Ch09 folder and play it.

The movie starts with the "Gameboy" in a robotlike entrance transformation, opening its cover revealing the two billboard images. Then the menu of six buttons comes in from the left. Finally the blue buttons and the two billboards become active as hot spot rollovers (see fig. 9.1).

The second example of advanced rollover buttons is the movie USA.dir. This movie is a United States menu panel, featuring a map of the United States with all the states as active rollover buttons (see fig. 9.2). Scripting USA.dir builds on similar techniques used in the Apple "Gameboy" movie but has more advanced functionality in its rollover buttons.

Open the movie USA.dir in Director from the Ch09 folder and play it.

Figure 9.1

Apple's home page Shockwave movie features dissimilar rollovers.

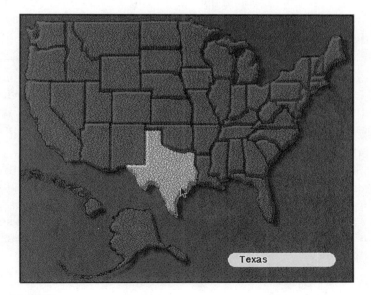

Figure 9.2

USA.dir has interlocking rollovers for each state. A detail map automatically pops up when you roll over the northeast.

USA.dir features the use of rollrover buttons in navigation. Just roll over the northeastern states and see how the rollover triggers a jump to a totally new frame. USA.dir also illustrates how using mouseCast enables you to create irregular and interlocking buttons. This can't be done by scripting the buttons with Lingo's rollover function. Before scripting rollover buttons you should weigh the pros and cons of scripting with the mouseCast function versus the rollover function.

Using the mouseCast versus the rollover Function

Before any button can be given rollover behavior, you need a handler to figure out which button is being rolled over. Either of the Lingo functions rollover or mouseCast can be used to detect which button is under the mouse. Once you evaluate the channel number of the button sprite under the mouse, you can change its location, castNum, color, or ink, or trigger any routine you want.

To refresh your memory, here is a summary of how Lingo's rollover function has already been used. The rollover function tests whether a particular sprite is being rolled on. To find out which button, if any, is currently being rolled on, you have to use the rollover function to test all sprite channels that have rollover buttons in them.

This is usually scripted using a "repeat with" loop. Typically, the repeat loop increments an index variable through all the button sprite channel values. Rollover is tested using rollover for each index number. When the loop in this reaches the channel of the sprite that is under the mouse, the rollover function returns a true value, and you have found your sprite.

This method works well, and is not hard to program, but it has two disadvantages. First, it can be a sluggish performer, especially with a large number of rollover buttons, as each must be individually tested with the rollover function. Second, the rollover function only tests whether the mouse is within the rectangular bounding box of the sprite. This is a problem for nonrectangular buttons, especially when your rollover buttons interlock on the stage.

Wouldn't it be nice if there were a function that instantly returned the sprite channel number of the sprite under the mouse? Perhaps a function called mouseSprite? Well, there is no such function in Lingo, but there is the mouseCast function. The mouseCast function is a handy Lingo command that returns the number of the cast member that is under the mouse. All you need is a way to figure out which sprite corresponds to that cast member returned by mouseCast, and voilà! the desired mouseSprite function has been improvised.

All that is required is establishing a simple linear relationship between the button cast and the matching button sprite. You can then use the mouseCast function to easily obtain the channel of the sprite under the mouse. So, building a linear structure into your cast and score is the way to use the mouseCast function to return the "mouseSprite." This mouseCast method takes more time on the front end in setting certain variables and insuring the linearity of button cast and score, but it enables you to overcome the previously mentioned disadvantages of using the rollover function.

Note

Pros of the mouseCast Method

Faster execution, even with lots of buttons.

Pixel-level button response, not just bounding box response. If the ink of the bitmapped button sprite is set to Matte ink, mouseCast only responds if over opaque pixels of the sprite. This is ideal for nonrectangular buttons.

Cons of the mouseCast Method

Longer setup time.

Not very modular. The linear structure of cast and score, which makes it all work, can be broken easily. If you move the offset location of the cast or the sprites, you have to change the magic offset variable accordingly. If the sequential order of cast and corresponding sprite channel is broken, the script won't function.

EXAMPLE 9-1:

Scripting with mouseCast: The Apple "Gameboy" Movie

The "Gameboy" movie was written for Apple to serve as a main menu for a shocked Web site. Thanks to their Online Communications group, we are able to highlight it here.

In the CD-ROM Ch09 folder there is a nearly completed version of Apple's Shockwave movie. It has been worked up to the point of arranging the rollover hot spots in the score. In this section, you perform the steps of laying out the score properly and initializing the global variables.

Shortcut

Open the file apple_x.dir from the Ch09 folder of the CD-ROM.

Setting Linear Button Structure

Here you arrange the button cast and score, and initialize the global variables in a way that is typical of the mouseCast technique of rollover buttons.

Setup of the Cast and Score

In apple_x.dir the objects that actually do the work are invisible QuickDraw rectangles positioned over the key areas of the stage. Areas of the stage that respond when rolled over or clicked on are called *hot spots*. Using a nonfilled, nonbordered QuickDraw rectangle is a common method of creating a hot spot.

1. Confirm that your hot-spot buttons are all in a row in the cast, as shown in figure 9.3. Notice how they are labeled. Labeling the buttons with sequential names helps avoid confusion.

    The first button cast member—45—is called BlueHot1.

    The remaining five blue-button hot spots are ordered and labeled correctly.

    The hot-spot buttons for the two billboards are in cast 51 and 52, labeled BillHot1 and 2.

Next, lay out your sprites in the score from lower to higher channel numbers in the same sequence as in the cast.

2. Open the score window and click in the cell at sprite channel 25, frame 120.

3. Select all the button cast members (45–52) in the cast window by clicking on cast 45, then Shift-clicking on cast 52.

Figure 9.3

Hot-spot buttons for apple x.dir.

4. Drag the selection from the cast window to the score window. Drop the selection into the cell at sprite channel 25, frame 120. This creates a stack of button sprites in frame 120 from channel 25 to 32. They are automatically in the correct order.

The next step is to arrange the hot-spot sprites over the correct locations on the stage. All the buttons are currently located at center stage.

5. Click and drag the topmost hot-spot button (sprite 32) directly over the right-hand billboard image.

6. Put sprite 31 over the left billboard.

7. Place sprite 30 (the top blue button sprite) so that it covers the text *Outside Resources* and its blue button.

8. One at a time, place sprites 29 through 25 in a similar fashion.

    Your hot spot buttons are now arranged on the stage correctly.

9. Duplicate frame 120. Mark a frame insertion point at frame 120 by clicking on the 2 of 120 in the frame number bar (under the marker channel). A blinking frame insertion point should appear.

10. Choose Score, Insert Frame to duplicate frame 120.

Your score should now appear exactly as in the score in figure 9.4.

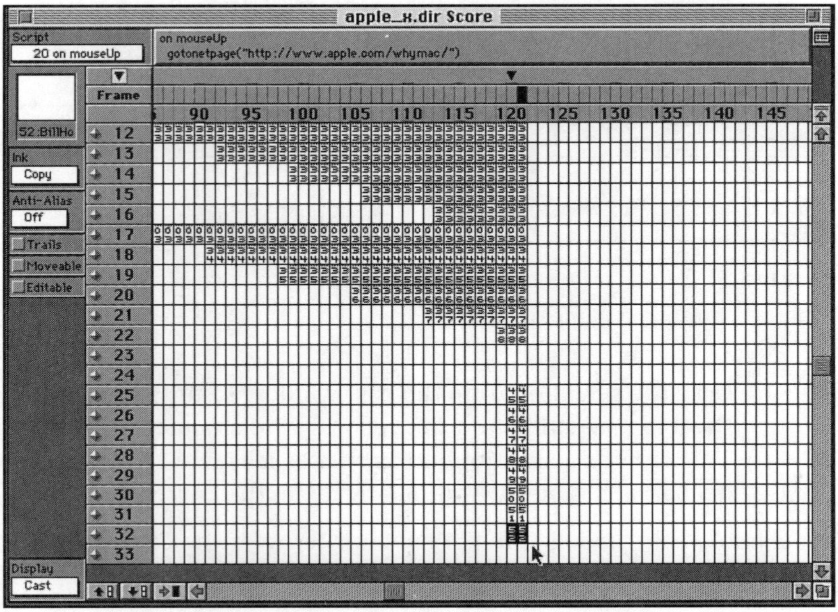

Figure 9.4
The score arrangement of the rollover hot spots.

Initializing Global Variables

You have just established a linear correspondence between the cast numbers and the sprite numbers of the hot spots. This enables you to control the button rollover behavior with the following scripts. You will now be taken through the scripting logic.

First you set global variables. There exists some magic number, which when added to the value of the mouseCast gives back the button's sprite channel number. This magic offset number must be set in a global variable when the movie starts.

Your global variables are initialized in the On startMovie handler, which is in the movie script (cast member 17).

1. You can get to the movie script in either of two ways. Choose Window, Script to open the script window, use the green arrows to scroll to cast 17, then open the movie script by double-clicking on it. Or, you can double-click cast 17 in the Cast window and the Script window will open to the movie script.

We have deliberately left two variables empty for you to set. The global variable gCastOffset corresponds to the cast number of the first hot-spot button.

2. Set 45 as the value for gCastOffset.

   The global variable gSpriteOffset corresponds to the lowest sprite channel containing the hot-spot sprites.

3. Set 25 as the value for gSpriteOffset.

   The global variable gMagicOffset is the numerical difference between gCastOffset and gSpriteOffset. This is the number you need to add to the mouseCast when you want to obtain the elusive "mouseSprite." If you are not sure why the gMagicOffset is set to (gSpriteOffset – gCastOffset) then take this as a little mental exercise to reason through.

   Your On startMovie script now looks like figure 9.5.

4. Press Enter to compile and close the script window.

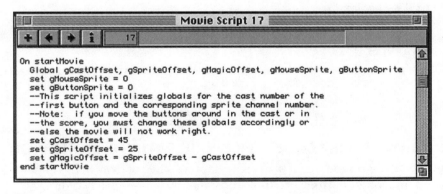

```
On startMovie
   Global gCastOffset, gSpriteOffset, gMagicOffset, gMouseSprite, gButtonSprite
   set gMouseSprite = 0
   set gButtonSprite = 0
   --This script initializes globals for the cast number of the
   --first button and the corresponding sprite channel number.
   --Note:  if you move the buttons around in the cast or in
   --the score, you must change these globals accordingly or
   --else the movie will not work right.
   set gCastOffset = 45
   set gSpriteOffset = 25
   set gMagicOffset = gSpriteOffset – gCastOffset
end startMovie
```

Figure 9.5

When you play the movie, Director excecutes the startMovie handler which initializes the global variables.

The checkButtonSprite Handler

The scripting has been broken down into three handlers, each of which is a conceptual step in bringing your rollover buttons to life. The checkButtonSprite handler identifies the sprite channel of the button under the mouse. Then, the checkButtonType handler identifies which kind of button you are dealing with. Finally, different behavior is assigned accordingly by the doButton handler.

The checkButtonSprite handler is shown in figure 9.6. This handler puts the number of the sprite under the mouse into the global variable gMouseSprite. First it gets the number of the cast under the mouse. Then it turns this number into the number of the sprite under the mouse by adding the gMagicOffset. Finally, if the "mouseSprite" is not a button sprite at all, it sets gMouseSprite to zero.

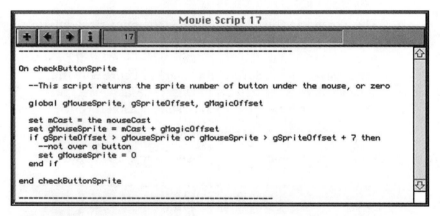

```
                        Movie Script 17
 +   ←   →   i        17

------------------------------------------------------------
On checkButtonSprite

  --This script returns the sprite number of button under the mouse, or zero

  global gMouseSprite, gSpriteOffset, gMagicOffset

  set mCast = the mouseCast
  set gMouseSprite = mCast + gMagicOffset
  if gSpriteOffset > gMouseSprite or gMouseSprite > gSpriteOffset + 7 then
    --not over a button
    set gMouseSprite = 0
  end if

end checkButtonSprite
------------------------------------------------------------
```

Figure 9.6
Set the global variable gMouseSprite to the sprite of the button under the mouse, or zero if no button is under the mouse.

Rollover Buttons with Dissimilar Behavior

In the button examples of previous chapters, the rollover behavior was the same for all buttons. In Apple's "Gameboy," there are two different types of rollover buttons: a menu of round blue buttons on the left and two square billboards on the right. Each button type has its own highlight sprite and therefore must be differentiated and handled separately.

The checkButtonType Handler

The checkButtonType handler is shown in figure 9.7. Its purpose is to distinguish between the two kinds of buttons. checkButtonType does this by testing for each button type according to which sprite channel is being rolled, and sets a global variable gButtonType accordingly. If the "mouseSprite" is in the lower range, then it is a blue button and gButtonType is set to 1. If the "mouseSprite" is in the upper range, then it is a billboard button and gButtonType is set to 2.

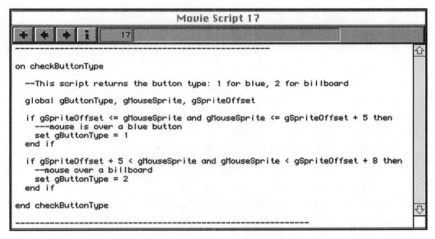

Figure 9.7

This script returns the button type: 1 for blue, 2 for billboard.

The doButton Handler

The second step when making dissimilar buttons, after checking button type, is to assign the correct behavior to the buttons. For this, you use the doButton handler.

The doButton handler is shown in figure 9.8. It tests each of the three possible button scenarios:

- ⚡ No button is under the mouse (both highlights off)

- ⚡ A blue button is under the mouse (blue on and billboard off)

- ⚡ A billboard button is under the mouse (billboard on and blue off)

Two different button highlight sprites are puppeted in frame one in sprite channels 23 and 24. The doButton handler positions these button highlight sprites on and off the stage as needed.

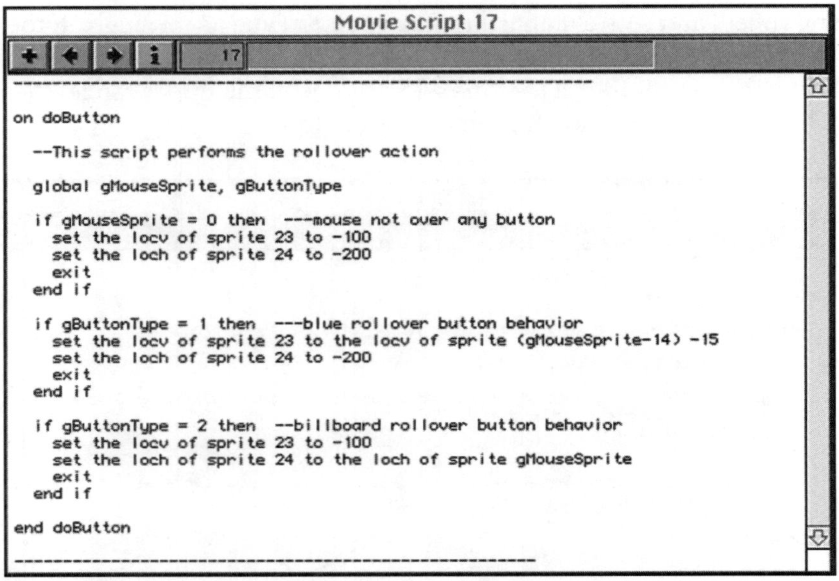

```
                          Movie Script 17
  +  ◄  ►  i      17
------------------------------------------------------------
on doButton

  --This script performs the rollover action

  global gMouseSprite, gButtonType

  if gMouseSprite = 0 then  ---mouse not over any button
    set the locv of sprite 23 to -100
    set the loch of sprite 24 to -200
    exit
  end if

  if gButtonType = 1 then  ---blue rollover button behavior
    set the locv of sprite 23 to the locv of sprite (gMouseSprite-14) -15
    set the loch of sprite 24 to -200
    exit
  end if

  if gButtonType = 2 then  --billboard rollover button behavior
    set the locv of sprite 23 to -100
    set the loch of sprite 24 to the loch of sprite gMouseSprite
    exit
  end if

end doButton
------------------------------------------------------------
```

Figure 9.8
This script performs the appropriate rollover action.

Calling the Handlers

The last steps of button scripting in the Apple movie is to call the button handlers.

1. Put a score script in frame 120 by double-clicking on the script channel of frame 120.

2. Enter the following script:

```
on exitFrame
   checkButtonSprite
   checkButtonType
   doButton
end
```

3. Put the following score script in frame 121:

```
on exitFrame
    checkButtonSprite
    checkButtonType
    doButton
    go marker (0)
end
```

4. Finally, put a marker in frame 120.

Rewind and play to see it work.

In this Apple movie, you saw how the rollover behavior was scripted in three steps. The operations performed by the three handlers could have been streamlined into a single handler for even faster execution speed. As an exercise, see if you can combine the functioning of the three handlers into a single handler. Then, in the score scripts in frame 120 and 121, replace the three sequential calls to the old handlers with a single call to the new streamlined handler.

EXAMPLE 9-2:

The USA.dir Movie

USA.dir takes rollover buttons to the next level of complexity by demonstrating interlocking buttons as well as navigation triggered by rollover buttons. As with the Apple "Gameboy" movie, USA.dir uses the mouseCast function to make it all work. As you will see, this advanced button scripting technique has many potentially powerful uses in Shockwave movies.

Nonrectangular Rollovers

Open the movie USA.dir in Director. Rewind and play, and try out the rollovers. Notice how responsive they are. The highlight changes as your mouse just crosses any part of the interlocking irregular borders of the states.

Using the mouseCast function enables you to have 40 rollover buttons, all live at one time in this movie. Try doing that using the rollover function! Like the Apple.dir movie, there is a one-to-one linear correspondence between button cast and sprites, making it possible to use the mouseCast function to return "mouseSprite."

Open the score and look at frames 2–6, as shown in figure 9.9.

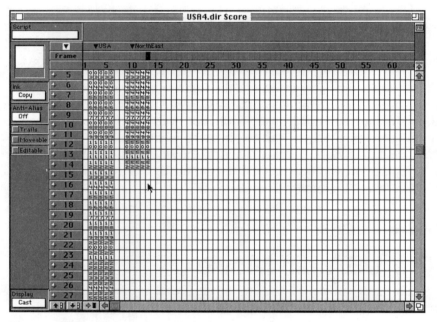

Figure 9.9

Many buttons are active at once in USA.dir. The linear button arrangement allows you to use the mouseCast function to script these rollover buttons.

The button behavior is scripted under the checkUSA and checkNorthEast scripts. In the checkUSA script, behavior is differentiated with one special case: the northeast. See the following section for discussion of the northeast case.

If the mouse is over any other state's sprite, it puppets that sprite, changes the colors, and restores the colors on the previously highlighted sprite, if any. Notice that Matte ink is applied to these sprites. Using Matte ink on the button sprites allows the mouseCast function to respond to their irregular shapes. Matte ink is a key ingredient in making nonrectangular buttons work.

In addition, Matte ink used on a closed 1-bit sprite enables you to apply both a foreground and background color and still get a nonrectangular border. It is like getting two colors for the price of one bit.

Tip

Using Matte ink on 1-bit sprites gives you much greater color control over the 1-bit sprites. The black pixels of the cast image are mapped to the sprite's foreground color, and white pixels to the background color. With this, you can simulate a dithered or duotone look, create nice gradients, or add more depth and texture using the lowly 1-bit cast. With clever use, Matte ink can make your 1-bit images look substantially like 8-bit.

The one setback with using Matte ink is transparency. The matte works properly only within areas of your bitmap that are completely encircled with black pixels. The areas of transparency are determined like water trying to flow to the interior of your bitmap. If there is a break in the black border, transparency will flow in as far as it can. All it takes is a one pixel leak and you lose your background color to the transparency flood. This also adversely affects mouseCast interactions, as mouseCast does not respond when over a transparent part of a sprite.

Finally, checkUSA tests to see if it is not over state at all. If it was just recently over one, it unhighlights, leaving no states highlighted at all.

Using Rollovers to Jump to Another Frame

USA.dir does more interesting things with rollovers. One obvious use is that it changes a text field to show the name of the state that is being rolled over.

Further, it shows how rollover buttons can be used to trigger navigation. In USA.dir, rolling over the northeast portion of the United States map causes a detail map to appear, as shown in figure 9.10. This is needed because there are some small states in New England that cannot be seen without a detail map.

Examine the script checkUSA in the movie script. A separate test handles the special case of northeast rollover, jumping the playback to the "NorthEast" marker. The background dims, and the detail map is super-imposed.

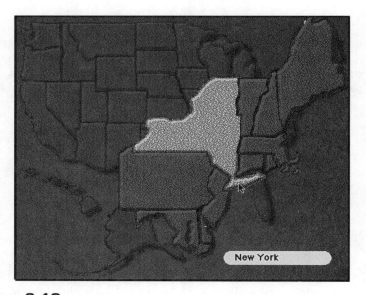

Figure 9.10

The North East detail map pops up when the northEast button is rolled over.

Once in the "NorthEast" loop, the rollover behavior must be scripted differently because you need a way back to the main USA map, and thus a different handler is called. The checkNorthEast handler is nearly the same as checkUSA.

The difference is in the special case testing. If the mouse is not over any of the detail states, then it must be over the background, or not on the stage at all. The special case of mouse over the background sends you back to the frame with the "USA" marker.

Tip

Another application of rollover-triggered frame jumping allows your movie to exceed the 48-sprite limit. If you have more buttons to display than available sprite channels allow, you can split the stage into two or more different zones. Each of these zones are like separate scenes in the score. They are visually identical, but each contains a subset of the total number of button sprites. You program rollover behavior to jump undetected across zones where appropriate.

In this chapter you have learned advanced rollover button techniques. This should be a good start in the right direction for constructing powerful, well-behaved, responsive, and innovative user interfaces for the Web.

In chapter 10, you learn more ways to use Lingo to enhance the interest of your shockwave movies. You create two new movies that serve as very versatile info-accents to your Web page.

PART IV

Lingo Is Your Friend

CHAPTER 10

Basic Shockwave Lingo

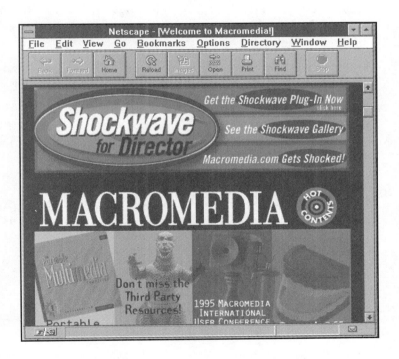

Many users are intimidated by Lingo, Director's scripting language. This is unfortunate, because Lingo is actually quite easy to learn. Lingo is, however, a very powerful tool that the Shockwave developer cannot get along without. Every example in this book contains some Lingo. We've already discussed rollovers and Go Tos. In this chapter you learn some more Lingo that every Shockwave developer needs to know.

EXAMPLE 10-1:

Under Construction

One of the most frustrating things about browsing the Web is the huge number of "under construction" notes and graphics strewn around. This movie gives you a way to lessen the sting of that frustration by adding a little humor to your site. It also demonstrates the usefulness of even small sound effects.

In this movie, a dump truck will drive onto the screen, dump out the word *construction*, and drive off. Then the word *under* will be lowered in on top.

Shortcut

The file you are creating is in the Ch05/Ex3 folder and is called undcon.dir.

Begin working in Director.

1. Choose File, Preferences, and set stage size to 96 pixels (width) and 24 pixels (height) and stage location to top 22 pixels.

2. Set the stage color to gray using the color chip on the lower right of the control panel.

3. Import the file dtruck.pic from the Ch10 folder.

4. With the lasso tool, select the bed portion of the cast member. Cut it and paste it into a new cast member.

5. Double-click on the marquee tool to select the new cast member. Choose Effects, Free Rotate. Rotate it approximately 55 degrees clockwise.

6. Without deselecting the rotated bitmap, choose Effects, Auto Distort. Type **3** in the text box to create three new cast members and press the Create button.

7. Go back to the first bed cast member. Using the registration tool, which is the tool with the crosshairs icon, click on the bottom right of the first bed cast member.

8. Click on the bottom right corner of each bed cast member.

Note

The registration point controls the placement of bitmaps on the stage. By placing the registration point on equivalent parts of each cast member, you can switch cast members without screwing up the placement.

9. Drag the truck body and the first bed cast member to frame 1, channels 2 and 3 of the score. Position the bed so that it is in its original position relative to the truck body.

10. Open the paint window and type **CONSTRUCTION** in 10-point Chicago Bold.

11. Using the marquee tool, select the *TION*, cut it out, and paste it into a new cast member.

12. Repeat with the *TRUC*.

13. In the score, drag the bed sprite to channel 5.

14. Drag the *TION* cast member onto the stage so that its top just protrudes above the top of the bed.

15. If the *TION* cast member isn't already in channel 3, move it there.

16. Select frame 1, channels 2–5 of the score.

17. Drag the sprites to the right edge of the stage.

18. In the score, Option-drag (Alt-drag in Windows) the sprites to frame 12. Position them slightly to the left of the center of the stage. Make sure you don't change the vertical position.

Here's where things get a little tricky.

19. Option-drag (Alt-drag) the truck-body sprite to frame 16.

20. In-Between Linear frames 12–16 in that channel.

21. Repeat the last two steps with the truck bed.

22. Select the bed sprite in frame 13. Select the first rotated bed cast member.

23. Choose Score, Switch Cast Members.

24. Select the bed sprite in frame 14. Select the second rotated bed cast member. Choose Score, Switch Cast Members.

25. Repeat with the next frame and the next cast member.

26. Option-drag (Alt-drag) the bed sprite in frame 15 to 16.

27. Select frame 16, channels 2–5 and Option-drag the sprites to frame 30.

28. Drag the sprites just off the left edge of the stage.

29. Select frames 16–30, channels 2–5 and In-Between.

30. In the cast, select the three cast members that are parts of the word *CONSTRUCTION* and choose Cast, Duplicate Cast Member.

31. Double-click on the first duplicate to open it in the paint window.

32. Double-click on the marquee tool and select Effects, Free Rotate. Rotate the bitmap approximately 55 degrees.

33. Press the right-arrow button in the paint window toolbar to move to the next cast member and repeat.

34. Repeat for the third part of the word. Your cast should look something like figure 10.1.

35. Position the playback head to frame 13.

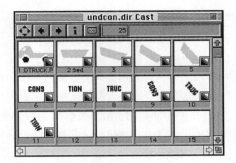

Figure 10.1
The cast with rotated text.

36. Drag the rotated *TION* cast member to the stage and position it about halfway up the tilted bed, as shown in figure 10.1. If the sprite is not in frame 13, channel 3, move it there.

37. Option-drag the sprite in the score to the next frame. Position it so that it is starting to slide down the tilted bed.

38. Repeat the previous step twice. By the fourth frame (number 16), the bottom corner of the sprite should be almost equal with the bottom of the wheels.

39. Drag the untilted *TION* from the cast into the score at frame 16, channel 6. Position it on the stage so that its bottom edge is vertically aligned to the bottom of the truck wheels (this imaginary line can be thought of as the ground). Horizontally, align the right edge with the bottom corner of the tilted sprite. You will have two versions of the *TION* overlapping. Drag the one in channel 6 to frame 17. Option-drag the sprite to channel 6, frame 66.

40. Select frames 17–66, channel 6. Choose Score, In-Between Linear.

41. Save the file as undcon.dir in the Ch10 folder.

Play the file. It should look like the truck dumps out the *TION* and drives off the screen.

42. Position the playback head at frame 22. Drag the tilted *TRUC* cast member onto the stage and position it as if it is half out of the back of the truck bed. Make sure the sprite is in channel 4.

43. Option-drag the sprite to frame 23. Position it on the stage so that it is almost all the way out of the truck.

44. Drag the untilted *TRUC* cast member into frame 24, channel 7. Position it so that it fits with the *TION* as though it is all one word.

45. Select frames 24–66, channel 7. Select Score, In-Between Linear.

46. Position the playback head at frame 27. Drag the tilted *CONS* cast member onto the stage and position it as if it is half out of the back of the truck bed. Make sure the sprite is in channel 4.

47. Option-drag the sprite to frame 28. Position it on the stage so that it is almost all the way out of the truck.

48. Drag the untilted *CON* cast member into frame 29, channel 8. Position it so that it fits with the *TRUCTION* as though it is all one word.

49. Select frame 31, channel 4. In the cast, select the third bed cast member. Choose Score, Switch Cast Members.

50. Select frame 32, channel 4. In the cast, select the second bed cast member. Choose Score, Switch Cast Members.

51. Select frame 33, channel 4. In the cast, select the first bed cast member. Choose Score, Switch Cast Members. Your score should look like figure 10.2.

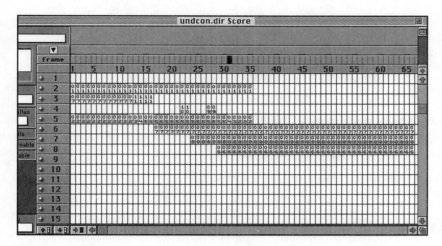

Figure 10.2

The score after the construction of *CONSTRUCTION*.

Now you need to lower the word *UNDER* onto the stage.

52. Open the paint window. Type **UNDER** in black 14-point Chicago Bold.

53. Drag the cast member into frame 41, channel 5 of the score.

54. On the stage drag it mostly off the top, directly over *CONSTRUCTION*.

55. Option-drag the sprite to frame 49 in the score. Position it on top of *CONSTRUCTION*.

56. Select frames 41–49 and In-Between Linear.

57. In the frame in which the sprite comes to its final position, use the line tool in the tool palette to draw a 2-pixel vertical line from the horizontal center of the sprite to the top of the stage. This is the cable being used to lower the UNDER sprite into position. Option-drag the sprite to the frame in which the top of the sprite first appears on the stage (roughly frame 46). Choose Score, In-Between Linear. Extend UNDER sprite from frame 49 through 66.

Now to give it some sway.

58. Select the UNDER sprite in frames 43 and 44 and press the right-arrow key once. Select the UNDER and cable sprites in frame 46 and press the left-arrow key once.

Save and play the movie. The truck should come onto the stage from right to left, dump out the word *CONSTRUCTION*, and drive off. Then the word *UNDER* should be lowered down.

What this movie needs now is some sound.

Adding Sound

1. Select File, Import. Select Sounds from the List Files of Type drop-down list. In the Ch10 folder on the CD, find truck.aif and squeak11.aif (these are edited sounds from Macromedia's clipMedia 1 CD), then choose Import All.

2. Select frames 2–38 in sound channel 1.

3. Select Score, Set Sound, then select truck.aif and choose OK.

4. Drag the squeak11.aif cast member into frame 41, sound channel 1. Select frames 41–56 of sound channel 1 and choose Score, In-Between Linear. Select Cast, Cast Member info and make sure that the "looped" option has been selected.

Save and play the movie; it's still a little flat. What you will now do is vary the sound of the engine according to what the truck is doing.

1. In the script channel in frame 1, click on the script bar and type the following script:

```
on exitFrame
  set the volume of sound 1 to 128
end
```

Director (and Shockwave) has two ways of controlling the loudness of sound. There is a global sound level, which controls the level of all sounds on the machine. This value goes from 0–7, and is the level you set when you use the Sound Control Panel on the Mac or a mixer utility on Windows. Messing with this setting is generally discouraged, especially with Shockwave movies. There's nothing more irritating than browsing the Web in a quiet office, only to have your machine suddenly blast out punk rock at top volume!

The second way to control loudness is the "volume of sound n" property. This is a number from 0–255, which is scaled by the global sound level, and can be set independently for each sound channel. In other words, if your global sound level is set at 6 and you set the volume of sound 1 to 128, the sounds in channel 1 will be half as loud as the system beep (approximately). If your sound level is at 3 and you set the volume of sound 1 to 255, it will be about the same loudness.

Tip

2. The truck begins to lift its bed at frame 12. Because the engine has to work harder to drive the hydraulics when it does this, it should get louder just before it starts to rise. In the score channel of frame 10, type the following script:

```
on exitFrame
   set the volume of sound 1 to 255
end
```

3. When it is done dumping out the letters, the engine should quiet down a little. Select the script channel in frame 17, and click on the script drop-down arrow at the upper left of the score window. Then select the script that sets the volume of sound 1 to 128.

4. After the truck leaves the stage, its sound should die away. So at frame 34, add the following script:

```
on exitFrame
   sound fadeOut 1, 120
end
```

Note

The second parameter in the sound fadeOut command is the time it takes in ticks to fade out. *Ticks* are Director's basic time unit: 1/60th of a second. So 120 ticks is 2 seconds. In this case the fadeOut is interrupted halfway through, as we shall see, but that is okay.

5. The squeak sound is a little softer than the truck noise, so crank up the volume on it. Copy the script from frame 10, and paste it into the script channel in frame 41.

Save the file.

Finishing, Burning, and Embedding the Movie

Now to add the final touches of Lingo. You will make the movie pause for 15 seconds at the end, then repeat.

1. In the script channel of frame 65, type the script:

```
on exitFrame
  startTimer
end
```

The startTimer command initializes a variable called "the timer," which simply keeps track of how many ticks have elapsed since the startTimer command was called.

2. In the script channel of frame 66, type the script:

```
on exitFrame
  if the timer < (15 * 60) then go the frame
  else go frame 1
end
```

This script checks to see whether 15 seconds have elapsed since the startTimer was called. If not, it simply repeats the frame. If so, it goes again to the beginning of the movie.

The movie is now done. Save the file.

3. Drag the movie onto Afterburner and save it as undcon.dcr in the Ch10/Movies folder.

4. In your text editor, open the ex10_1.html file.

5. In the line before the `<table>` tag, insert the following lines:

```
Please be patient, this site is
<p>
<embed src="Movies/undcon.dcr" height=40 width=128>
<p>
```

Open the file in your browser. The movie should play, with sound, and repeat roughly every 20 seconds. The next example explains how to color sprites on the fly.

EXAMPLE 10-2:

News Flash!

At times you will want to inform people who browse your page that you have some news you want them to see. This movie, newsflsh.dir, draws attention to that item of news.

The main new technique in this movie is the use of Lingo to color sprites. This is a powerful technique that can make movies much more interesting.

Creating the Movie

Begin in Director.

1. Set the background color in the control panel to a medium gray.

2. Choose File, Movie Info and choose the System-Windows palette in the Default Palette popup. Open File, Preferences, and set the stage size to 96×24.

3. Open the paint window. With the text tool, type N in black 18-point Courier Bold.

4. Click on the + button in the paint window toolbar to create a new paint cast member.

5. Type e with the same text style. Click on the + button again and repeat the process for all the characters in *wsFlash!*.

6. Select all the cast members and choose Cast, Transform Bitmap. Change the color depth to 1 bit and choose OK. Choose OK to the warning message.

7. Drag the *N* cast member into the score in frame 5, channel 4 and position it approximately one-fourth of the way from the left edge of the stage.

8. Place the *e*, *w*, and *s* cast members in successive channels.

9. Select channels 4–7 (which should have, in order, the *N*, *e*, *w*, and *s* sprites in them), frames 5–15. Choose Score, In-Between Linear.

10. Select frames 5 and 6, channel 5. Press the Delete key.

11. Select frames 5–8, channel 6. Press the Delete key.

12. Delete frames 5–10 of channel 7.

13. Save the file as newsflsh.dir in the Ch10 folder.

Your stage and score should now look like figure 10.3, with the letters coming in as if typed.

You now need to add Flash!, but first you need to make room for it.

14. Select channels 4–7 in frame 15. Option-drag (Alt-Drag in Windows) them to frame 20. Select Score, Sprite Info and set the Distance from Left Edge of Stage to 2.

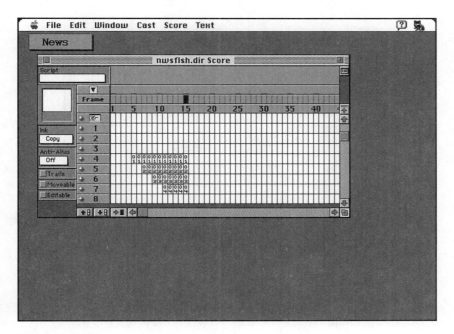

Figure 10.3

The stage and score with the first half of NewsFlash!.

15. Select frames 15–37 of these channels and select Score, In-Between Linear.

16. Drag the *F* cast member into the score at frame 21, channel 8. Position it so it looks like it is part of the same word as News.

17. Repeat with the *lash!* in successive channels.

18. Drag the *l* 2 frames forward.

19. Drag the *a* 4 frames forward, the *s* 6 frames, the *h* 8 frames, and the *!* 10 frames. In the ink pop-up, select Background Transparent. Your score should look like figure 10.4.

20. Select channels 8–13, frames 21–37 and choose Score, In-Between Linear.

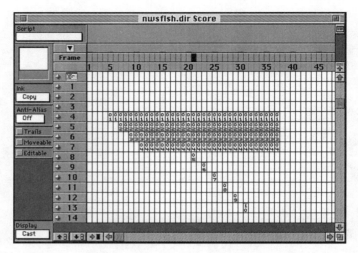

Figure 10.4
Preparing to In-Between.

Save and play the movie.The letters should appear to be typed.

Now it is time to add sound.

1. Choose File, Import.

2. Select Sounds in the List Files of Type drop-down list, and import teletype.aif. This is an edited version of another file found on Macromedia's ClipMedia 1 CD.

3. Select the cast member you just imported and Choose Cast, Cast Info. Check the loop check box.

4. Select frames 5–32 in the sound channel. Choose Score, Set Sound and choose the teletype file (which should be your only choice).

The final step is to add random colorization of the letters.

1. Select the script channel in frame 36. Click on the script bar and type the following script:

```
on exitFrame
  repeat with i = 4 to 13
```

```
      puppetSprite i, true
   end repeat
end
```

Note

The puppetSprite command causes the sprites to ignore the score and be controllable by Lingo. You need to puppetSprite the sprites now because their foreground color is black in the score, and you need to be able to set that value.

2. In the script channel of frame 37, type the following script:

```
on exitFrame
   set the forecolor of sprite (random(10)+3) to
   ➥(random (256) -1) "1)"
   go the frame
end
```

This script chooses a random letter sprite and sets its foreground color to a random entry in the current palette. Then it simply goes to the same frame, which will then draw the sprite in its new color.

3. Save the file.

4. Drag the file onto Afterburner.

5. Save it as newsflsh.dcr in the Ch10/Movies folder.

6. In your text editor, open the ex10_2.htm file. Before the new product announcement, but after the **<p>**, add the line **<embed src="Movies/newsflsh.dcr" height=24 width=96>**.

Open the file in your browser. The text should be typed in as before, only with the accompanying sound. At the end, the text should change color randomly.

This chapter has introduced you to Lingo. The next chapter enables you to expand your knowledge of the scripting language.

CHAPTER 11

Animating with Lingo

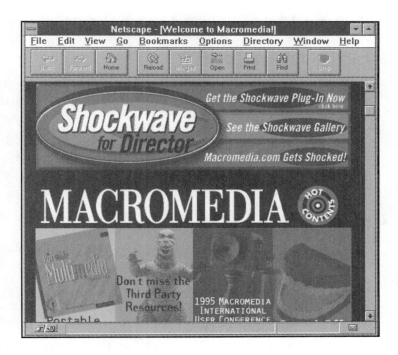

Although Lingo intimidates many Director users, it is a tool that can expand the capabilities of the program by many orders of magnitude. With Lingo, you can respond to the user's actions as well as the whims of chance. We have already seen how Lingo can respond to the user's mouse over an object and also to a mouse click. Lingo, however, can do much more. In this chapter you explore some ways to animate with Lingo, as well as ways to follow the cursor with a sprite. Neither of these examples may seem to be of immediate utility, but they should serve to introduce you to the basics of Lingo animation, as well as give you some ideas for your own animations.

Both examples in this chapter use the same spinning ball animation. The first example shows you how to bounce that ball around the screen, and the second shows how to follow the cursor with it.

EXAMPLE 11-1:

Bouncing Ball

This example covers the basics of moving sprites around with Lingo. You also use the sprite intersects function to make sure the ball does not go off the screen.

First you lay out the movie (a very simple process), then you add the code to move the ball around, then the code to keep it on the stage, and finally, a randomizing function to add variety to the movie.

Laying Out the Stage

The layout for this movie is very simple. A benefit of this simple layout is that changing the stage size requires at most two steps, which means a similar movie can be adapted for a variety of uses.

1. Open Director and choose File, Preferences. Set the stage size to 400×300 pixels.

2. Choose File, Movie Info and set the default palette to System-Windows.

3. In the control panel, set the stage color to a light gray.

We set the stage color to a light gray because the spheres were created with a white background. The edge pixels of the sphere picts, therefore, are a very light color. You could easily add a tiled background image to the movie to add visual interest—in fact we have left channel 1 open for you to do just that—but if you do, it should be a light color. To get the cleanest image, you should create your art with a background color as close as possible to the color over which the image will be composited. This is especially true when creating antialiased text in Photoshop, but it's a good general rule as well.

4. Choose File, Import, then select file type of Macintosh PICT if in Windows and navigate to the Ch11/Pix directory.

5. Choose Import All to import all the sphrxx.pic files.

6. In the tool palette, set the foreground color to the same gray as the stage color, select the line tool, and set the line width to 1 pixel.

7. With the Shift key held down, draw a line across the top edge of the stage.

8. Select the sprite in the score and choose Score, Sprite Info or Command+K (Control+K in Windows).

9. Set the width of the sprite to 400, the height to 1, the distance from the left edge to the stage to 0, and the distance from the top edge also to 0.

10. Option-drag (Alt-drag in Windows) the sprite to the next channel. Choose Score, Sprite Info again and set the distance from the top of the stage to 299.

11. With the Shift key held down, draw a line along the left edge of the stage. Choose Score, Sprite Info again and set the height to 300, the width to 1, and the distances from the top and left edge of the stage to 0.

12. Option-drag the sprite into the next channel and choose Score, Sprite Info yet again. The only value you need to change is the distance from the left edge of stage, which should be set to 399.

13. Select all four sprites and drag them so that they are in channels 2–5.

14. Select channels 2–5, frames 1 and 2 and choose Score, In-Between Linear.

15. Finally, drag cast member 1 into frame 1, channel 10 of the score. Choose Score, Sprite Info one more time. Make sure Background Transparent is selected in the ink popup.

16. Set the distance from the left edge of stage to –100.

Note

You move sprite 10 off the stage because its initial position will be set by Lingo, depending on how big the stage is, and it's better to have the sprite first appear in the correct position, instead of having it jump from some arbitrary position to the center of the stage.

Save the file as spinme.dir in the Ch11 folder. Your cast and score should look like figure 11.1

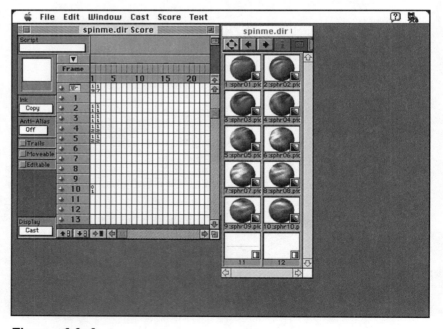

Figure 11.1

The stage appears blank because you will be moving the spinning ball with Lingo.

Moving the Ball

To move the ball, you will puppet it, then add an X and Y movement. You also need to cycle the cast members to make it spin.

1. To control any sprite with Lingo, you need to make it a puppet. You also need to set the sprite's initial position, which, for our purposes, will be the center of the stage. So select the script channel in frame 1 and click on the script bar. Type the following script:

```
on exitFrame
  puppetsprite 10, TRUE
  set the locH of sprite 10 to (the stageRight
  ➥ - the stageLeft)/2
  set the locV of sprite 10 to (the stageBottom
  ➥ - the stageTop)/2
end
```

Each sprite has a location, expressed in two variables: the locH (horizontal) and the locV (vertical). You set the vertical and horizontal locations of the sprite to halfway between the edges.

Note

The stageRight, the stageLeft, the stageTop, and the stageBottom are the boundaries of the stage expressed in absolute coordinates. So if the stage window is 16 pixels from the left edge of the monitor and 400 pixels wide, the stageLeft is 16 and the stageRight is 416. This is somewhat confusing because the location of a sprite is expressed relative to the stage. So a sprite at the left edge of the stage is going to have a locH of 0, regardless of where the stage is located in the monitor.

2. In this script, you also need to set the initial velocity of the sprite, which is a random value. Because Director does not have vector variables, you will express the velocity in two global variables, dX and dY. To make these variables global and give them initial values, add the following line at the beginning of the script:

```
global dX, dY
set dX = random(7) - 4
set dY = random(7) - 4
```

The random function returns a number between 1 and the number specified—in this case 7. You subtract 4 so that the result is a number between –3 and 3. These numbers are arbitrary, but if the dX or dY gets too big, they can cause problems, as we shall see.

3. Close the script. Now you need to make the sprite actually move. Select the script channel in frame 2 and click on the script bar. Type the following script:

```
on exitFrame
  workFrame
  go the frame
end
```

This script merely calls the workFrame handler, which does the work, then loops and calls it again.

4. Click on the + button of the script window toolbar to create a new movie script. Type the following script:

```
on workFrame
  global dX, dY
  set the locH of sprite 10 to ((the locH
  ➥ of sprite 10) + dX)
  set the locV of sprite 10 to ((the locV
  ➥ of sprite 10) + dY)
  if the castnum of sprite 10 = 10 then set
the castnum of sprite 10 to 1
  else set the castnum of sprite 10 to
  ➥ ((the castnum of sprite 10) + 1)
end
```

The first line specifies that the dX and dY referenced in this script are the global ones, which have values already set from the previous frame. The next two lines add the value of dX and dY to the locH and locV of the sprite, respectively. The next line checks to see whether the number of the cast currently assigned to the sprite is 10, which is the last one in the sequence. If it is, the script assigns the first cast member in the sequence; if not, the next line assigns the next cast member in the sequence to the sprite.

5. Close the script. In the control panel, set the tempo to 90 frames per second. This will make the animation smoother.

6. Save the file. If you get a warning `The movie may not play correctly because one or more of the scripts have not been compiled`, click on Cancel, then choose Text, Recompile All Scripts (see the following Note). Then choose Save again. Run it, and the ball should spin off the edge of the stage. Run it a couple more times; it should go in a different direction each time.

Note

Director compiles Lingo scripts to get better performance. *Compiling* is the process of converting the English-like syntax of Lingo into something more machine-friendly. When you close a window, Director compiles the script that is currently in the window. When you move back and forth between scripts without closing the window, however, Director does not compile anything except the script that is showing when the window is closed. When you play the file or press the return key when the message window is frontmost, Director recompiles all the scripts in the movie. Saving, however, does not recompile, and the application warns you if you save with uncompiled scripts. Unless you are low on memory, therefore, when you get the warning message, it is always a good idea to cancel the save, then choose Text, Recompile All Scripts. If you do not do this, and then run a movie through Afterburner, the scripts may not work.

Checking for Boundary Conditions

Although the ball spinning off the stage is a nice effect and shows that Lingo can be used to animate things, it is not particularly interesting. You will now use the lines you drew at the borders of the stage to keep the spinning ball on the stage. You do this by checking to see if the ball intersects the border sprites.

1. Select Text, Find Handler and double-click on the workframe handler. Open the script in frame 2 by double-clicking on the script channel.

2. Add the following line right before the last line of the script:

    ```
    checkBounds
    ```

3. Underneath the workFrame script, add a blank line, then type the following script:

```
on checkBounds
  global dX, dY
  repeat with i = 2 to 3
    if sprite 10 intersects i then
      set dY = -1*dY
      set the locV of sprite 10 to ((the locv
      ➥ of sprite 10) + 2*dY)
    end if
  end repeat
  repeat with i = 4 to 5
    if sprite 10 intersects i then
      set dX = -dX
      set the locH of sprite 10 to ((the locH
      ➥ of sprite 10) + 2*dX)
    end if
  end repeat
end
```

This script first tests to see if the ball intersects the top or bottom border sprites. If so, it reverses the vertical component of the ball movement. Then it sets the ball away from the wall so that the dY will not be reversed again. It then does the same thing with the left and right borders, reversing the horizontal movement this time.

Save and run the movie. The ball should bounce around in a fairly deterministic manner.

Adding Variety to the Ball's Motion

Although the ball's motion so far is somewhat realistic, it isn't as interesting as it could be. In this section you add a randomize handler to change the ball motion slightly, and invoke it whenever the ball hits a wall. The probability that the ball will change velocity is author-defined, and is contained in the changeFreq variable. The velocity will change one every changeFreq times, so the larger the variable, the less likely the velocity is to change.

1. In the frame 1 exitFrame handler, add changeFreq to the list of global variables. The line should read as follows:

```
global dX, dY, changeFreq
```

2. Somewhere in the handler add the line:

```
set changeFreq = 3
```

The value of changeFreq is arbitrary, but 3 is a good initial value because it allows reasonably realistic movement while still adding some variety. Close the script and open the movie script.

3. Select Text, Find Handler, checkBounds handler. Below the checkBounds handler add the following handler:

```
on randomize
  global dX, dY, changeFreq
  if random(changeFreq) = 1 then set dX  =
  ➥ dX + random(3) - 2
  if random(changeFreq) = 1 then set dY  =
  ➥ dY + random(3) - 2
  if abs(dX) > 8 then set dX = 8*(dX/abs(dX))
  if abs(dY) > 8 then set dY = 8 * (dY/abs(dY))
end
```

This script makes a random check to see if it should change dX, and then checks for dY. If either check results in 1, it adds –1, 0, or 1 to the appropriate variable.

The script then checks to see if the absolute value of dX is more than 8 (in other words, if dX is more than 8, or less than –8), and if so, sets it to 8 times the value of dX divided by the absolute value of dX. If dX is negative, dX/abs(dX) will produce –1; otherwise, it will produce 1. So, if dX is less than –8, the script will set dX to –8, and if more than 8, the script will set dX to 8.

4. Now you have to actually invoke the randomize handler. In the checkBounds handler, add the following line before each of the end ifs:

```
randomize
```

The checkBounds handler should now read as follows:

```
on checkBounds
  global dX, dY
  repeat with i = 2 to 3
    if sprite 10 intersects i then
      set dY = -1*dY
      set the locV of sprite 10 to ((the locV
      ➥ of sprite 10) + 2*dY)
      randomize
    end if
  end repeat
  repeat with i = 4 to 5
    if sprite 10 intersects i then
      set dX = -dX
      set the locH of sprite 10 to ((the locH
      ➥ of sprite 10) + 2*dX)
      randomize
    end if
  end repeat
end
```

Finally, you will invoke the randomize function when the user clicks the mouse on the ball.

5. Select frame 1, channel 10 in the score.

6. Click on the script bar and type the following script:

```
on mouseDown
  randomize
end
```

We use mouseDown because it is hard to click down and up on a moving object.

Save the file and run it. The ball should bounce around, and when the user clicks, it should change direction.

Embedding the File in an HTML Document

1. Drag the file onto Afterburner and save it as spinme.dcr in the Ch11/Movies folder.

2. Open the file ex11_1.htm in your text editor. Add the following line anywhere in the document:

   ```
   <embed src="Movies/spinme.dcr" width=400 height=300>
   ```

3. Save the file.

Open the file in your browser. The movie should act just like it did in Director. Next, we will make the spinning ball follow the cursor.

EXAMPLE 11-2:

Follow the Cursor

In this example you learn how to make a sprite follow the cursor. We will also introduce trails, a feature of Director that, when used well, can be a great boon to the Shockwave developer. It is important to note, though, that trails have some strange characteristics and can have unforeseen side effects, which are detailed later.

You will be using the same spinning sphere graphics from the last example. First you make the spinning sphere follow the cursor, then you make it draw copies of itself when the mouse button is pressed.

Following the Cursor

First, import the graphics and set the location and the cast member.

1. Open Director, and choose File, Preferences. Set the stage size to 400×300 pixels.

2. Choose File, Movie Info and set the default palette to System-Windows.

3. In the control panel, set the stage color to a light gray.

4. Choose File, Import, then select file type of Macintosh PICT if in Windows and navigate to the Ch11/Pix directory.

5. Choose Import All to import all the sphrxx.pic files.

6. Drag the sphere into the score in channel 10, frame 1. Set its ink to Background Transparent.

7. Choose Score, Sprite Info and set the distance from the left edge of stage to −200.

8. Drag a rectangle the same color as the stage across the whole stage. Choose Score, Sprite Info and make sure it covers the whole stage. If it is not in channel 1 in the score, move it there. Select channels 1–10, frames 1–2 and choose Score, In-Between Linear.

9. Select the script channel of frame 1. Click on the script bar and type the following script in the script window:

```
on exitFrame
  puppetsprite 10, TRUE
end
```

10. Close the script window and double-click on the script channel in frame 2. Type the following script:

```
on exitFrame
  workFrame
  go the frame
end
```

11. Now click on the + button in the script window toolbar to create a new movie script. Type the following script:

```
on workFrame
    set the locH of sprite 10 to the mouseH
    set the locV of sprite 10 to the mouseV
    if the castnum of sprite 10 = 10 then set the
    ➥ castnum of sprite 10 to 1
    else set the castnum of sprite 10 to the
    ➥ castnum of sprite 10 + 1
end
```

The first two lines of the script simply set the horizontal and vertical location of the sprite to the horizontal and vertical location of the mouse. The mouseH and the mouseV are built-in Director variables.

The second two lines should be familiar from the last example. They simply swap in the appropriate new cast member for the sprite.

12. Close the script window. In the control panel, set the tempo to 90 frames per second. Save the file as follow.dir in the Ch11 folder.

Play the file. You should see something similar to figure 11.2.

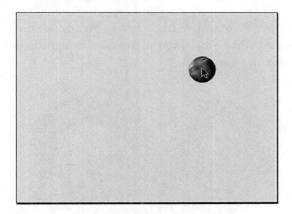

Figure 11.2
The sprite follows the mouse around the stage.

Using Trails

Trails are a feature of Director that can provide some interesting effects, but can also cause problems if used incorrectly. In this section, you will use the trails feature to paint on the stage.

The trails property of a sprite is set in the score, but because we want it to be totally controlled by Lingo, we will ignore that setting.

1. Select frames 1 and 2, channel 10 in the score. Click on the script bar and type the following script:

```
on mouseDown
  set the trails of sprite 10 to TRUE
  set the visible of sprite 1 to false
end
```

Note that the handler is on mouse**Down**, not the default mouseUp. We use mouseDown because we want the trails to turn on while the user is holding down the mouse button.

The script sets the trails property of the sprite to TRUE and sets the visibility of the stage-color rectangle to false. The reason for these settings will soon be apparent.

2. Play the movie, clicking and dragging the mouse around. Note that when you release the mouse button, a square area is cleared when you drag the mouse through the images, as shown in figure 11.3.

Figure 11.3
The bounding rect of the ball sprite erases the trails.

3. Now, add the following handler in the same script:

```
on mouseUp
  set the trails of sprite 10 to false
  updateStage
  set the visible of sprite 1 to TRUE
end
```

This handler is executed when the mouse button is released. It first turns off the trails property of the sprite. It then executes an updateStage command, which actually turns off the trails of the sprite. Finally, it sets the visibility of the stage-color rectangle on, which forces Director to redraw the whole stage (and therefore erase all the trails images).

Note

The updateStage command forces Director to redraw the stage, with updated sprite properties. Going to a frame has the same effect, except that any non-puppeted sprites will also be updated. UpdateStage redraws only the effects of any changes that are made with Lingo.

Close the script window, save the file, and run it.

Embedding the Movie

1. Drag the file onto Afterburner.

2. Save it as follow.dcr in the folder Ch11/Movies.

3. Open the file ex11-1.htm in your text editor.

4. Change the `<embed>` line you added in the last example to read:

   `<embed src="Movies/follow.dcr" width=400 height=300>`

5. Open the file in your browser. Move the mouse around within the movie and note the cursor following the mouse. Experiment with clicking and dragging.

This chapter has introduced you to the basics of animating with Lingo. In the next chapter, you explore the possibilities of non-standard-shaped movies.

PART V

Exotica

CHAPTER 12

Vertical Movies

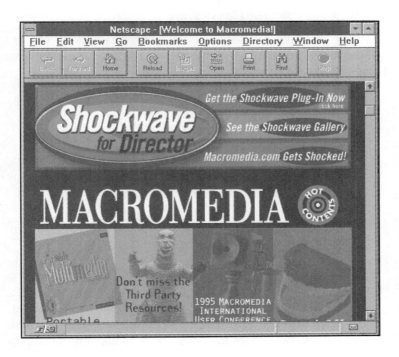

B ecause of the influence of television and film, we often expect moving images to be wider than they are tall. The aspect ratios of 4:3 and 16:9 are implicit in our expectations of the appearance of moving images. There is no reason why the creative Shockwave developer, however, should limit herself to movies that follow those aspect ratios. Director and Shockwave provide the freedom to make movies of any shape, as long as it's rectangular.

This chapter explores two movies that use a highly vertical shape to add interest and variety to Web pages. The first example, a vertical title, is an example directly from our Web site. There is no reason why page titles need to be a line across the top of the screen, and this example provides an alternative. The second example is another control panel, but vertical this time, which frees the user from having to scroll all the way to the bottom or top of the page to use the navigation features you have so thoughtfully included in your site.

These examples are not meant to be exhaustive, but rather to provide food for thought, and to provoke you to think of more creative ways to use the power of Shockwave.

EXAMPLE 12-1:

Vertical Title Animation

In this example you use looping background tiles and text rendered in Photoshop to make a simple title animation.

Creating the Text in Photoshop

1. Open Photoshop. Choose File, New and set the size of the new file to 32×448 pixels.

2. Click on the black-and-white icon below the foreground/ background color chips on the tool palette (see fig. 12.1). This sets the foreground color to black and the background to white.

3. If the background color of the image is not white, choose Select, All or Command+A (Control+A in Windows) to select the entire image. Then press the Delete key to clear the image.

The black-and-white icon.

Figure 12.1
Clicking on this icon sets the foreground color to black and the background to white.

> When you clear an area in Photoshop, it fills the cleared space with the background color.
>
> **Tip**

4. Select the text tool and click near the top of the image.

5. In the Type Tool dialog box, select the Centered Alignment radio button (the second one in the left column). Deselect the Anti-Aliased check box. Choose a sans serif font with a heavy weight, one that would make a good headline font. (This example uses Helvetica Black.) Set the size to 30. In the text entry box, type `Related Links`, with a return between each letter. Choose OK.

> We use the centered alignment with a return between each letter rather than the vertical alignment setting because the vertical alignment does not center the letters in the column.
>
> **Note**

The letters will probably not be distributed over the whole image. There are two ways to handle this: adjusting the leading or centering the letters vertically. We used leading.

6. Press Delete to clear the type and click on the image with the text tool again.

7. Specify 34 in the Leading text box. Choose OK.

8. Position the text so that it is centered horizontally.

9. Save the file as other.pic.

Animating the Texture in Director

Your first task is to make the background textured. For this, you'll switch from Photoshop to Director.

1. Choose File, Movie Info and set the default palette to System-Windows. Choose File, Preferences and set the stage size to 32×448.

2. Choose File, Import, then navigate to the Ch12/Pix folder and choose Import All. These are the texture cast members.

3. Choose File, Import. Navigate up one level and import the file other.pic you just created.

4. Option-drag the 10 texture cast members into the score in frame 1, channel 1. The first 10 frames will be selected.

5. With frames 1–10 still selected, choose Score, Sprite Info or Command+K (Control+K in Windows) and set the distance from the top and left edges of the stage to 0.

6. Option-drag (Alt-drag in Windows) the 10 texture cast members into the score again, this time in frame 1, channel 2. The first 10 frames will be selected.

7. Choose Score, Sprite Info again and set the distance from the top of the stage to 64 (the height of the tile).

8. Repeat with channels 3–7, increasing the distance from the top of the stage by 64 pixels each time.

9. Now select frames 1–10, channels 1–7 and Option-drag (Alt-drag in Windows) the whole chunk to frame 11, channels 1–7. Repeat until frames 1–60 are filled. Save the file in the Ch12 folder as related.dir.

10. We want to loop through one cycle of the background at the end of the movie, so click on the script channel in frame 60 and type the following script:

```
on exitFrame
  go marker(0)
end
```

go marker(0) goes to the previous marker in the score. Because you have not yet added any markers to the score, this script will not be of much use yet.

11. Drag a marker (the triangle above the word *Frame* in the upper left of the score) out to frame 51. Your score should now look like figure 12.2.

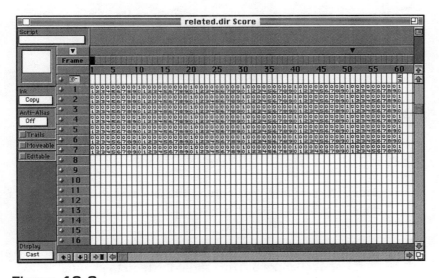

Figure 12.2
The background pulses to add visual interest to the title.

Save the file, then run it. Note how it loops at the end.

Animating the Text

The text will enter by sliding from the left, one character at a time.

1. Select the paint text cast member. Choose Cast, Duplicate Cast Member 11 times, creating one cast member for each letter.

2. Open the first paint text cast member. Use the marquee tool to select all the letters except for the first one. Press Delete to clear them.

3. Press the forward arrow button in the paint window toolbar to move to the next cast member. Select the first letter with the marquee tool and clear it. Select all the remaining letters except for the *e,* which is at the top of the remaining letters. Clear them.

Tip

We are creating a cast member for each letter by duplicating the entire word and then removing all the extraneous letters because we want each letter to use the word for placing its registration point, not the single letter. When you create a new bitmap cast member—whether by duplicating an already existing one, importing a bitmap, or drawing a new one—Director gives it a registration point in the center of the bitmap. That is all well and good, normally, but because you already have the correct spacing in this instance, it would be additional work to replicate that. By duplicating the entire word, each cast member keeps a registration point relative to the word. So when you drag them all onto the stage (as you will shortly), they will be appropriately spaced.

4. Repeat the process for each letter, though not for the space between words.

5. Move the script in the score to the end and shift the letter cast members one to the left so that they are all adjacent. Save the file. Your cast should now look like figure 12.3.

6. Select all the letter cast members and drag them into the score in frame 1, channel 8. They should extend to channel 19. With all the letter cast members still selected, select the "ghost" ink effect.

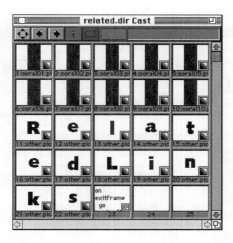

Figure 12.3
The letters are ready to be placed on the stage.

7. Drag the sprite in channel 8 to frame 4, the sprite in channel 9 to frame 7, the sprite in channel 10 to frame 10 and so on, with each sprite 3 frames farther than the one in the previous channel. When you are done, your score should look like figure 12.4.

8. Select the first letter sprite and Option-drag it to frame 1 of its channel (number 8). Choose Score, Sprite Info and set the distance from the left edge of stage to negative the sprite width. If the sprite is 20 pixels wide, for example, set the distance from the left edge of the stage to –20.

Warning

Confusingly, the Sprite Info dialog box ignores the registration point and uses the upper left corner of the bounding box of the sprite. This means that the value returned in Lingo for the location of a sprite does not match the sprite info values, and it means that changing the registration point of a bitmap will change the sprite info values, even though the sprite has not moved.

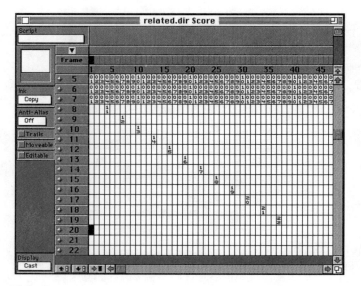

Figure 12.4
The letter sprites are distributed every three frames.

9. Select the letter sprite in channel 9 and drag it to frame 4. Repeat the Sprite Info process.

10. Repeat with the rest of the letter sprites, dragging them three frames back, then setting their horizontal position off the stage.

11. Select channels 8–19, frames 1–60 and choose Score, In-Between Linear. Your score should look like figure 12.5.

Save and run the file. The letters should slide in one-by-one and then hold while the background pulses.

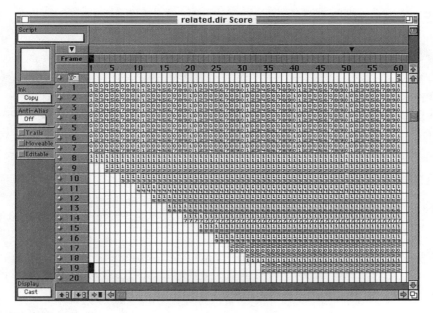

Figure 12.5
The final score layout includes the letters sliding onto the stage one by one.

Embedding the File in an HTML Page

1. Drag the file onto Afterburner.

2. Save it in the Ch12/Movies directory as related.dcr.

3. Open the file in your text editor and add the following line immediately before the `<img>` line:

```
<embed src="Movies/related.dcr" align=left height=448
width=32 border=3>
```

Save the file and open it in your browser. Next you create a vertical movie that functions as a control panel.

EXAMPLE 12-2:

Vertical Control Panel

This control panel has many of the same features as the example in chapter 6. It is vertical, however, and so has somewhat of a different effect. In this example we use a different method of highlighting sprites we roll over.

Assembling the Movie

1. Open Director. Choose File, Movie Info and set the default palette to System-Windows. Choose File, Preferences and set the stage size to 32×192.

2. Choose File, Import, then navigate to the Ch12/Pix2 folder and choose Import All. These are the texture cast members, as well as the button cast members.

 Note

The cast members must be reorganized in the cast window because they are organized alphabetically. Reorganize the cast so the button cast members and the texture cast members are separated.

3. Select the button cast members (home.pic, info.pic, shock.pic, and who.pic) and choose Cast, Transform Bitmap. Set the color depth to 1 bit. Choose OK and ignore the warning message.

4. Select all the texture cast members and Option-drag (Alt-drag in Windows) them into the score. Choose Score, Cast Info and set the distances from the left and top edges of the stage to 0.

5. Option-drag (Alt-drag) them into the score again and set the distance from the top edge of the stage to 64. Repeat and set the distance to 128. You now have the texture background.

6. Drag the home.pic cast member onto the stage near the top, centered horizontally.

7. Drag the shock.pic cast member onto the stage, also horizontally centered, below the home graphic.

8. Repeat with the who.pic and info.pic graphics. Select all the
    button cast members (channels 4–7). Set the foreground color
    in the tool palette to red (color number 6 in the Windows
    system palette). Your stage should look like figure 12.6.

Figure 12.6
The button cast members are distributed evenly down the stage.

9. Select channels 1–3, frames 1–6. Option-drag them to frames
    7–12. Select channels 4–7, frames 1–12. Choose Score, In-
    Between Linear. With channels 4–7, frames 1–12 still selected,
    select Background Transparent in the ink effects. You now
    have the basic layout for the movie; now you have to add
    interactivity.

Adding Interactivity

You add goToNetPage functionality to the control panel, as well as make
the buttons blue when the mouse passes over them.

1. Drag a marker out to frame 6. Select the script channel in
    frame 10. Type the following script:

```
on exitFrame
  checkFrame
  go marker(0)
end
```

2. Select the script channel in frames 6–9. Type the following script:

```
on exitFrame
  checkFrame
end
```

3. Now select an empty cast member in the score, then choose Window, Script or Command + O (Control + O in Windows) and type the following script:

```
on checkframe
  global gLastRoll
  repeat with i = 4 to 7
    if rollover (i) then
      if i <> gLastRoll then
        set the forecolor of sprite i to 1
        set the forecolor of sprite gLastRoll to 6
      end if
      set gLastRoll = i
      exit
    end if
  end repeat
  set the forecolor of sprite gLastRoll to 6
  set gLastRoll = 47
end
```

This is the standard rollover script that you've seen several times before, with one exception. Instead of moving around a highlight sprite, you change the color of the selected button. To do this, however, you need to add the following script in frame 1:

```
on exitFrame
  repeat with i = 4 to 7
    puppetsprite i, true
  end repeat
end
```

This script enables Lingo to set the foreground color of the sprites, instead of the score asserting its settings.

Finally, you need to add the goToNetPage functionality:

4. Option-Control-click (Alt-right-click in Windows) on the home cast member to open the cast member's script. Type the following script:

```
on mouseUp
   goToNetPage("../home.htm")
end
```

5. Close the window and Option-Control-click on the info.pic cast member. Type the script:

```
on mouseUp
   goToNetPage("../info.htm")
end
```

6. Repeat with the other button cast members, going to shock.htm and who.htm respectively.

Embedding the File in the Web Page

1. Drag the file onto Afterburner. Save it as vpanel.dcr in the Ch12/Movies folder.

2. Open the files home.htm, info.htm, shock.htm, and who.htm in your text editor.

3. After the <h2> line, add the following line in each file:

```
<embed src="Movies/vpanel.dcr" height=192 width=32
➥ border=3>
```

Open one of the files in your browser. Play with the control panel. Clicking on the appropriate icon should send you to that page.

In the next chapter you create a game using Lingo.

CHAPTER 13

Games

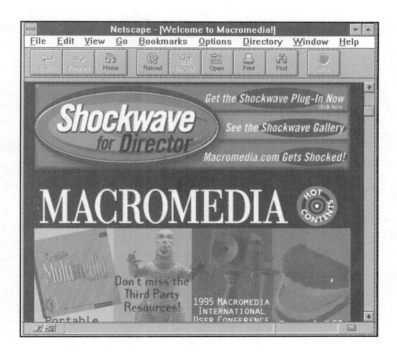

S hockwave is an excellent tool for making small games. Already, there are many games on the Web created using Shockwave. In this chapter you make a small game, which is admittedly of limited interest, but can serve as a way to attract people to your site. It also has a hidden feature. If the user scores 5 points, the user goes to a special hidden page.

EXAMPLE 13-1:

Catch the Blob

This game builds on the bouncing ball movie you made in Chapter 11, "Animating with Lingo." You replace the spinning ball with a wallowing blob, and you give the user a box in which to catch the wallowing blob. You then make the blob change color as the score gets higher or lower, and finally make the user win or lose, depending on the score.

Replacing the Spinning Ball

You begin in Director.

1. Open the file spinme.dir in the Ch11 folder and save it as game.dir in the Ch13 folder.

2. Select cast members 1–10 (the spinning-ball cast members) and choose Edit, Clear Cast Members.

3. Select cast 1, open the paint window, set the foreground color to black, and draw a blobby-looking thing, roughly 40×40 pixels. Click on the + button on the paint window toolbar to make a new cast member. Draw another blobby thing about the same size. Repeat three more times. Select all five new cast members and Choose Cast, Transform Bitmap. Set the color depth to 1 bit and the size to 40×40. Your cast should now look like figure 13.1.

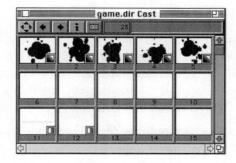

Figure 13.1

Five blobs replace the spinning globe.

4. Because the blob has only 5 cast members, rather than the 10 the bouncing ball had, you need to readjust the scripts accordingly. Choose Text, Find Handler and double-click on workFrame in the list box.

5. The fifth line of the workFrame handler currently reads:

```
if the castnum of sprite 10 = 10 then set the castnum of
➥ sprite 10 to 1
```

Because the blob has only 5 cast members, you need to change the maximum cast number to 5. The line should now read:

```
if the castnum of sprite 10 = 5 then set the castnum of
➥ sprite 10 to 1
```

Save the file and run it. The blob should bounce around like the ball did in example 11-1.

Adding Interaction

You now need to add some interaction to actually make the movie a game.

1. Select the unfilled rectangle tool in the tool palette.

2. Make sure the foreground color is black and the line width is 1 pixel. With the shift key held down, draw a square on the stage. In the score, move the rectangle to frame 1, channel 9. Choose Score, Sprite Info and set the width and height to 60 pixels. Set the horizontal location to −100 pixels. Choose OK.

3. In the score, Option-drag (Alt-drag in Windows) the sprite into frame 2 of the same channel.

You now need to make the square follow the cursor.

4. Open the score script in the first frame. After the line that reads `puppetsprite 10, TRUE` add the following line:

```
puppetsprite 9, TRUE
```

5. Now open the workFrame handler again. Before the line you recently changed, add the following two lines:

```
set the locH of sprite 9 to the mouseH - 30
set the locV of sprite 9 to the mouseV - 30
```

Because the registration point of a QuickDraw shape is its upper left corner and you want to center the square around the cursor, you need to correct for half the width and height of the square. This is why you subtract 30 from the mouse location. The entire script should now read:

```
on workFrame
  global dX, dY, changeFreq
  set the locH of sprite 10 to ((the loch of sprite 10)
  ➥ + dX)
  set the locV of sprite 10 to ((the locv of sprite 10)
  ➥ + dY)
  set the locH of sprite 9 to the mouseH - 30
  set the locV of sprite 9 to the mouseV - 30
  if the castnum of sprite 10 = 5 then set the castnum
  ➥ of sprite 10 to 1
  else set the castnum of sprite 10 to the castnum of
  ➥ sprite 10 + 1
  checkBounds
end
```

6. Save and run the movie. Notice how the square follows the cursor around.

For aesthetics, and for your edification, you will change the cursor from the standard pointer to a small crosshair shape.

7. Select cast slot 7 and open the paint window. Draw two black, 15–pixel-long lines that cross at the center. Double-click on the color depth indicator to open the Transform Bitmap dialog box and set the color depth to 1 bit.

8. Close the paint window and open the frame 1 score script. Add the following line:

```
cursor[7,7]
```

The cursor command takes one or two parameters. The first parameter is the cast number of the cursor picture; the second parameter is the mask for the cursor. (The Director manual has more information about this command.) One pitfall that is easy to run into is that the cast members must be 1-bit.

Save and run the file. Figure 13.2 is a screen shot of the running movie.

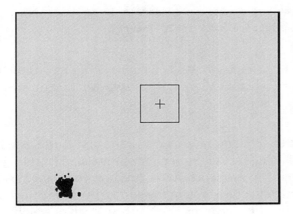

Figure 13.2
The cursor is now a crosshair.

Scoring

1. Select the blob sprites (frames 1 and 2, channel 10) and set the color of the sprites to the ninth color in the third-from-bottom row. This is smack in the middle of a series of nine reds that shade from bright red to almost black.

2. The object of the game is to click the mouse when the blob is entirely within the box. Fortunately, Lingo makes this easy. Add the following handler to the same movie script that contains the workFrame handler:

```
on mouseDown
  global gScore
  if sprite 10 within 9 then
    set gScore = gScore + 1
    beep
    randomize
  else
    set gScore = gScore -1
  end if
  if gScore = 5 then go "win"
  else if gScore = -5 then go "lose"
  set the forecolor of sprite 10 to 216 + gScore
  put gScore into field "score"
end
```

Putting a mouseDown in a movie script means the handler gets called any time there is a mouseDown that does not trigger any other script.

The sprite within function returns true if the first sprite listed is entirely within the bounding rect of the second sprite listed. In this case, if it is, you want to add 1 to the score. And if it is not, you want to subtract 1, beep, and change the direction of the sprite (by calling the randomize handler you created in chapter 11). You also declare a global variable in which to keep the score. Next you test to see if the score is either 5 or –5, and go to the appropriate frame (which you have yet to create) if it is. You next change the color, making it redder as the user gets closer to losing, blacker as the user gets closer to winning. The final thing you do is update the score display field (which also doesn't exist yet).

1. Because we made some assumptions in the previous script, we need to cover ourselves before trying to run it. Set the playback head to frame 2. Select the text tool in the tool palette and click on the stage. Set the font to 24-point Helvetica Bold. Size the text box so that it will contain two digits of that size. Choose Text, Border, 1 Pixel. In the cast, name the cast member "Score."

2. Drag a marker out to frame 10. Name it "win."

3. Open the paint window and type **You win!** in a fancy font. Drag the cast member into frame 10. Click on the script channel in frame 10 and type the following script:

```
on exitFrame
  GoToNetPage("../secret.htm")
end
```

4. Drag a marker out to frame 15. Name it "lose." In the script channel, add a go-to-the-frame script. Open the paint window and type **You Lose...To play again, click on the text**.

5. Drag that cast member into frame 15 of the score. Select the sprite and type the following script:

```
on mouseUp
  go frame 1
end
```

6. Select the sprites in frames 1 and 2, channel 10. You will notice they have a script. You want this to go away, so select 0 in the script pop-up in the upper left of the score window.

7. The last script change you need to make is initialization of the score variable. Open the frame 1 score script, add the gScore variable to the list of globals, then add the following two lines:

```
set gScore = 0
put gScore into field "score"
```

This resets the score variable and makes sure the display variable is reset as well. The frame 1 score script should now read as follows:

```
on exitFrame
  global dX, dY, changeFreq, gScore
  set gScore = 0
  put gScore into field "score"
  set dX = random(7) -4
  set dY = random(7) -4
  set changefreq = 3
  puppetsprite 10, TRUE
  puppetsprite 9, TRUE
  cursor[7,7]
  set the locH of sprite 10 to (the stageRight - the
  ➡ stageLeft)/2
  set the locV of sprite 10 to (the stageBottom - the
  ➡ stageTop)/2
end
```

8. The final change you need to make is the addition of a background. Import the file tile.pic from the Ch13 folder. Double-click on it to open the paint window, and choose Paint, Tiles. Click on the Use Cast Member button and click through until you have the tile.pic selected. Set the size to 64×64. In the tool palette, select the filled rectangle tool and select line width of 0 and the tile from the tile pop-up. Drag out the rectangle so that it covers the whole stage in channel 1 and Option-drag (Alt-drag in Windows) the sprite to frame 2.

Save the file and run it to test it. If you win, you should get an error.

Embedding the File in the HTML Document

1. Drag the file onto Afterburner.

2. Save it as game.dcr in the Ch13/Movies folder.

3. Open the file ex13_1.htm in your text editor.

4. Add the following line:

```
<embed src="Movies/game.dcr" width=400 height=300>
```

Save and open in your browser. Notice that when you score more than 5 points, the movie goes to the secret.htm page.

This chapter has shown you an example of how to make a simple game with Director. In the next chapter you explore some of the new, Shockwave-specific Lingo.

CHAPTER 14

Net-Specific Lingo

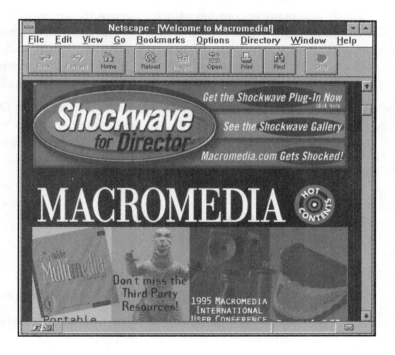

S hockwave is not simply Director on the World Wide Web. Macromedia has also added some Net-specific Lingo, called Lingo Network Extensions, to aid Web developers in making Shockwave a full citizen of the Internet. You have, in fact, used one of the Net-specific commands: GoToNetPage, beginning in chapter 6.

This chapter demonstrates an example of an animated graph using three of the new Lingo commands. There is a complete reference to the Lingo Network Extensions in appendix B.

EXAMPLE **14-1**:

Graphing on the Fly

One of the advantages of the Web is that information can be updated quickly and made accessible without the trouble involved in publishing and distributing paper copies of the information. One advantage of paper reports that is often lost, however, is graphs and charts that explain the numbers. The process of generating graphs to illuminate numbers that change daily or even hourly is cumbersome at best, impossible at worst.

This example is a simple application that plots a bar graph of up to five values. It uses three new Net-specific Lingo commands: getNetText, netDone, and netTextResult. First you create the (admittedly somewhat rudimentary) art, then add graphing functionality, and finally embed the file in an HTML page.

Creating the Pieces

This is the easy part of this movie.

1. Open Director.

2. Choose File, Preferences. Set the Stage Size to 400×300.

3. Choose File, Movie Info. Set the Default Palette to System Windows.

4. Set the stage background color to a light gray.

5. Open the paint window. Select the filled rectangle tool and set the foreground color to red.

6. Draw a rectangle approximately 200 pixels high by 50 wide. Set the foreground color to black and draw a 15-pixel-wide rectangle right next to the first rectangle; begin it at the bottom of the first rectangle and extend it to approximately 20 pixels from the top of the first rectangle. The cast member should look like figure 14.1.

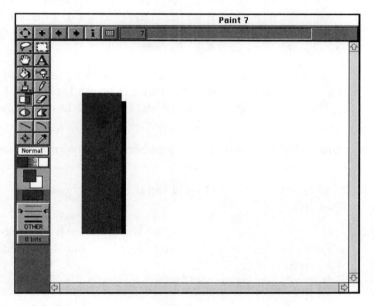

Figure 14.1
The bar for your bar graph.

7. Open the text window and set the font to 24-point Palatino Bold. Type **Retrieving Data....** While the text window is still open, click on the + button in the text window toolbar to create a new text cast member. Type a space, and name the cast member "title". Choose Text, Alignment, Center. Close the text window.

Tip

Typing a space in an empty text cast member forces the cast member to retain the text settings (in this case 24-point Palatino Bold) when new text is put into it. Otherwise, it will end up in 10-point Monaco or something equally generic.

8. In the cast window, select cast number 11. Choose Window, Text to display the text window. Set the font to 14-point Palatino Bold and type a space. Choose Cast, Duplicate Cast Member four times.

9. Cast members 11–15 should now be text cast members. Drag the Bar cast member into the score in frame 1, channel 11. Option-drag (Alt-drag in Windows) the sprite to channels 12–15.

10. Select all the sprites and choose Score, Sprite Info, then set the horizontal location to –100

11. Select cast members 11–15. Drag them into the score in channels 21–25.

12. Choose Score, Sprite Info and set the distance from the top edge of the stage to 270 and the distance from the left edge of the stage to –100.

13. Drag the Title cast member to the top of the stage and drag it out so it extends almost all the way across the stage. Drag the sprite to channel 9, frame 4. Option-drag it to frame 5 of the same channel.

14. Drag the "Retrieving Data" cast member into channel 10, frame 2. Select all the sprites and set their ink to Background Transparent. Save the movie as graphme.dir in the Ch14 folder. Your score should look something like figure 14.2.

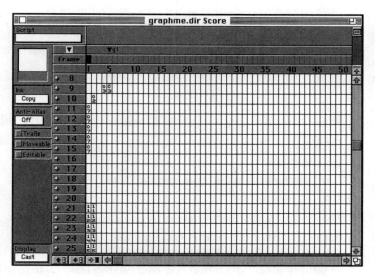

Figure 14.2

The score layout is prepared for some serious puppet spriting.

Adding Graphing Functionality

1. Select the script channel in frame 1, click on the script bar, and
   type the following script:

```
on exitFrame
  getNetText("../test.txt")
  repeat with i = 11 to 15
    puppetsprite i, true
    puppetsprite (i+10), true
  end repeat
end
```

This handler puppets sprites 11–15 (the bar sprites) and 21–25
(the value label sprites), but first it performs a getNetText
command.

Note

The getNetText command is new to Shockwave and starts the retrieval of a text item. Because the speed of a Net connection is uncertain (at best!), Shockwave does not require you to wait for the command to finish.

2. Now select the script channel in frame 3 and type the following script:

```
on exitFrame
  if netDone()=false then go the frame - 1
end
```

The netDone() function tests to see if the last network command (getNetText, in this case) is completed. If not, it goes to the previous frame. You go to the previous frame here, instead of simply looping, so that the "Retrieving Data..." text will flash, providing an indication to the user that something is going on.

3. Next, select the script channel in frame 4, click on the script bar, and type the following script:

```
on exitFrame
  put netTextResult() into graphtext
  set graphlist = []
  put line 1 of graphText into field "title"
  set j = the number of items in line 2 of graphText
  repeat with i = 1 to j
    append graphList, value(item i of line 2 ¬
    ➥ of graphText)
  end repeat
  set vScale = 200/max(graphList)
  set hScale = 350/j
  set v1 = 50
  set v2 = 250
  set leftMargin = 25
  repeat with i = 1 to j
    set the text of cast (10 + i) to string
    ➥ (GetAt(graphList,i))
    set the rect of sprite (10 + i) to rect((hScale*¬
    (i-1)+leftMargin), v2, (hScale*(i-1)+leftMargin)+ v1,¬
```

```
      v2- (vscale * GetAt(graphList,i)))
      set the locH of sprite (20+i) to ¬
      (hScale*(i-1)+leftMargin)+ v1/4
      puppetTransition 4, 2, 2
      updatestage
    end repeat

  end
```

When a getNetText command is complete, the function netTextResult( ) contains the result of the call. You put that result into a variable, then initialize a list. You have defined the text item to consist of a title line, then a line of up to five values, separated by commas. The title line, unsurprisingly, you put into the "title" text cast member. Next, you walk through the second line of the text variable, converting each item to a numeric value, and tacking it onto the end of the list.

You have about 200 pixels of vertical space for the graph. Because you don't have any idea of the values' range, you scale the graph vertically by dividing the total height by the maximum value you have to graph. You scale it horizontally simply by dividing the width by the number of values.

v1 is the width of each bar, scaled to allow for some space between the bars even if there are five bars. v2 is the distance from the top of the stage at which the graph starts. You set it at 250 (50 pixels from the bottom) to allow for labeling the values underneath the bars.

You set the left margin at 25, which allows space between the ends of the graph and the edges of the stage.

The second repeat loop is the heart of this handler. It first sets the text of the label for the current item to a string of the number in the current item in the list.

Next, it sets the dimensions of the current bar sprite by setting the rect of the sprite. Setting the rect of the sprite scales the sprite to the size of the rect. Next, it moves the label underneath the current bar. Finally, it sets up a puppetTransition—in this case, a wipe up—and then calls an updateStage.

A puppetTransition does not actually occur until an updateStage is called or the playback head moves. You call the updateStage within the repeat loop so that the stage updates for each bar, which makes them wipe up one by one.

4. The final step is to add a go to the frame in the last frame of the movie to keep the stage updated. Save the movie.

Embedding the Movie and Creating the Graphed Data

1. Drag the movie onto Afterburner and save it in the Ch14/Movies folder.

2. Open the ex14_1.htm file in your text editor. Add the following line:

```
<embed src="Movies/graphme.dir" width=400 height=300>
```

3. Save the file. Open a new file in your text editor and type the following lines:

```
Our Company's Stock:
25,29,34,38,42
```

4. Save the file as test.txt in the Ch14 folder.

Open the ex14_1.htm file in your browser. See the graphing action!

You can play around with the values and the title in the text file to your heart's content.

By now you should have the tools to create your own Shockwave movies. The next chapter, which is the last, includes some information about where Shockwave is going in the future, as well as some speculation on the Net in general.

CHAPTER 15

What Does the Future Hold?

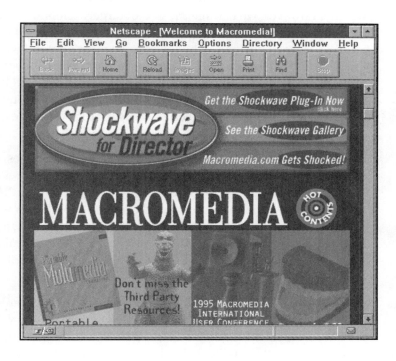

No discussion of such a new technology would be complete without some final notes on the future. Because Shockwave depends on the Internet, we first discuss upcoming issues regarding new methods of access. Secondly, we deal with the future of Shockwave, specifically, and then close with some final words. We hope that this chapter will give you some food for thought (or action) as well as a glimmer of the direction things are heading.

Big Pipes: Big Opportunities, Big Dangers

The future is an exciting place, and as a Shockwave developer you are poised to take it by storm. Most of the techniques you have learned in this book are intended to help you make the most of scarce bandwidth. Already, however, we can see the end of largely telephone-based Net access. As the pipes into the home and into businesses get faster and fatter, the extremely limited bandwidth we must contend with today will largely be a thing of the past. It is important to realize, however, that although bandwidth will become more available, it will still be limited. The inherent efficiency of Shockwave as well as the techniques you have learned from this book will still be necessary to produce responsive, truly Net-friendly content.

The recent discussion of Network Computers, set-top boxes, and the like is another reason you as a Shockwave developer should feel confident. Macromedia is strongly committed to their "Author Once, Play Any-where" strategy, which emphasizes the adaptation of Director playback on virtually any platform. Shockwave is an example of this, as is the 3DO player and several other upcoming players from Macromedia. You can be certain that as new platforms become available, Macromedia will give you the ability to play back Director movies on them.

The potential audience for a Web-based Shockwave production is gargantuan. With the approximately 15 million users of Netscape world-wide already plugged into the World Wide Web as a starting point, the demand for interactive, rich media of Shockwave movies will be tremendous. This is an audience that can be reached virtually free of the overhead and return rates that plague the CD-ROM industry.

Shockwave is an amazingly exciting tool. It can make a qualitative difference in delivering your message—artistic, political, and/or commercial—over the Internet. As pioneers in the field of Internet multimedia, however, we have both the privilege and responsibility of determining the direction this new technology takes the Web. The Internet is potentially the most powerful and democratic method of communication to arise since Gutenberg came up with movable type. Unlike television, there is little difference between the tools needed to make a Web page and the tools needed to view it. Shockwave has the power to increase the power of the Web without changing that balance significantly. Alternatively, it could play an unfortunate role by drastically increasing the amount of flash and glitter without adding any substance.

Deregulation and Privatization of the Internet

As someone who provides content for the Internet, you need to be aware of the changes approaching. There are two main factors that may make the Internet of six months or two years from now nearly unrecognizable: deregulation and privatization.

Currently, almost all personal access to the Internet is through the phone system. The Telecommunications Deregulation bill recently passed in Congress would allow cable companies, long-distance companies, even utility companies to compete for the right to provide higher-speed access to homes and businesses. This could mean cheaper, higher-speed access to the Internet for many people; however, it will almost certainly mean that large segments of the population will be left out of any new standards. What made the telephone a nearly ubiquitous instrument of communication was a policy called *universal access,* which required telephone companies to provide lifeline service, or very low-cost rates, to low-income people. This is why the telephone is so powerful: nearly everybody has one (at least in the U.S.). Under new regulations, however, companies setting up new networks are not only without obligation to provide lifeline service, but are free to wire only areas that they deem desirable. This will mean many areas, particularly low-income and rural areas, will be without high-speed access to the Internet.

Although the physical infrastructure of the Internet was largely funded by tax money, there has been a rush to privatize the system. What changes this will cause are as yet unclear, but because somebody has to make a profit in a privatized system, it will likely mean higher rates for access and maybe even per-bit charges on data transmission. An early example of the hazards of privatization is the introduction of a $50 charge for registering a domain name. There are undoubtedly many more to come, as well.

Despite the recent staggering growth of the Internet, only 2–3 percent of the U.S. population has access to the Web.

How Macromedia Is Making Shockwave Better

The possibilities for Shockwave are endless. But Macromedia has committed to two excellent features for the second release of Shockwave: audio compression and streaming. The addition of these two features will make Shockwave an even more powerful tool.

Audio Compression

In the current release of Shockwave, adding audio to your movie is a serious commitment. At 11 KB a second, audio can count for the majority of the size of your movie. A 100 KB movie with no sound will often compress to 40 KB, whereas a 100 KB movie of which half the size is audio will only compress to 70 KB! This is true whether the sound is extremely dense or mostly silence punctuated with other sounds. In the next version of Shockwave, Macromedia will be adding audio compression, which will allow much more extensive use of sound. How much compression we will be able to gain is yet to be determined, but in a 28.8 Kbps world, we'll take whatever we can get.

Streaming

In the current version of Shockwave, the user must wait for the entire movie to load before it begins to play. This is necessary because the Shockwave plug-in has no control over which chunks of the file the server will send first. In future versions, however, the author will be able to control which parts of the movie are loaded and in which order. This probably will not be similar to the feature in the current version of Director, in which the author specifies Before Frame 1, After Frame 1, or As needed for the cast loading in the Movie Info dialog box. Because the Internet is undependable at best, the author will probably have to provide for error recovery. The exact method of streaming is only speculation, and Macromedia may find a way to completely surprise us, but the capability to begin playing the movie before the entire cast is downloaded will add more flexibility for the Shockwave developer.

Final Words

Director has grown from an application designed for the Mac 128 to one that can take advantage of the latest Power Macintoshes and Pentiums. You can depend on Shockwave to scale just as well. As the Web grows and high-speed connections become more common, the value of a skilled Shockwave developer will rise, not decline. Already, leading CD-ROM developers are looking to the World Wide Web as the publishing medium of the future.

Now that you have learned the Shockwave basics and some techniques to make the most of the platform, you are well-positioned to play a leading role in the (wide) world of Web-based multimedia. We look forward to seeing the ways you use Shockwave.

PART VI

Appendixes

Basic Quick Reference

This appendix contains several useful items that will give you some easy-to-refer-to tools to use as you create Shockwave movies. There are three checklists: Starting a New Director Movie, File Size Reduction, and Things to Avoid. There is also a reference for the **embed** HTML command. Finally, as a special bonus, we have added a table of download times over various connections, courtesy of Macromedia.

Checklist for Starting a New Director Movie for Shockwave

⚡ Set default palette to System-Windows in the Movie Info dialog box (choose File, Movie Info).

⚡ Set your monitor's color depth to 256 colors (8-bit) if you are using a Macintosh.

⚡ Set your stage to the desired height and width in the Preferences dialog box (choose File, Preferences). All other preferences are overridden when you compress the file in Afterburner.

File Size Reduction Checklist

⚡ Remove all unused cast members from the cast.

⚡ Only use very short sounds sampled at 8 bits, 11.025 KHz, mono.

⚡ Reduce the bit depth of bitmapped cast members as far as possible; 1 bit is preferred.

⚡ Use QuickDraw objects for all lines, circles, rectangles, and textures.

⚡ Reduce large textured areas to a mosaic of tiled bitmaps if possible.

⚡ Use ink and color effects and scaling instead of adding cast members.

Checklist of Things to Avoid in Your Movies

⚡ Functions other than tempo settings in the time channel don't work.

⚡ Palette cycling is tweaky and annoying to most users.

⚡ Don't use nonstandard audio sampling rates (use 11.050 or 22.1 KHz only).

⚡ Don't use linked Media.

⚡ Make sure any QuickDraw text in your movie uses only standard fonts.

⚡ Don't use xObjects—they are not supported in Shockwave.

⚡ Don't use file I/O commands.

Writing HTML for Shockwave— Quick Reference

The HTML tag to embed a Shockwave movie is:

```
<embed>
```

The parameters are as follows:

Parameter	Description	Example
src	url of the movie	src="Movies/movie.dcr"
height	height of the movie	height=300
width	width of the movie	width=400

When writing HTML for shocked Web pages, remember to specify the height and width of the movies. This speeds up the layout of the page and omitting this can have unpredictable effects.

Finally, embed no more than five Shockwave movies in a single page and avoid multiple movies with audio on the same page.

New Lingo for Shockwave—Quick Reference

Several new commands are available for accessing the network from Director Lingo scripts. This appendix lists each of these new commands and functions and explains their usage.

Because the network is essentially an asynchronous place—that is, it takes time to get things from the Net, and in the meantime, Director can continue to interact with the user—most of the network commands involve starting an operation, checking to see if it has completed, then getting the results. This is different than most Lingo commands, which immediately return the result.

Three commands are available to start asynchronous operations, and one to preload into cache. Note that a URI (uniform resource identifier) is a more general specification than a URL (uniform resource locator), but for practical purposes they can be considered identical.

⚡ **GetNetText** *uri*
This command starts the retrieval of an HTTP item, to be read by Lingo as text. The uri parameter is a uniform resource identifier that specifies the HTTP item to be retrieved. At present, only HTTP URLs are supported as valid uri parameters.

⚡ **PreloadNetThing** *uri*
This command starts preloading an HTTP item into the local file cache. The uri parameter is a uniform resource identifier that specifies the HTTP item to be referenced. At present, only HTTP URLs are supported as valid uri parameters.

In general, an item that has been preloaded can be accessed immediately, because it is taken from the local disk cache rather than from the network. However, it is impossible to determine when an item may be removed from the local disk cache.

Two functions allow a Lingo script to determine the state of the asynchronous operation:

⚡ **NetDone()**
This function returns true when the asynchronous network operation is finished. Until that point, it returns false.

⚡ **NetError()**
This function returns the empty string until the asynchronous network operation is finished. Then it returns "OK" if the operation completed successfully or a string describing the error if it failed to complete successfully.

After an asynchronous operation has finished, three functions are available to retrieve the results:

⚡ **NetTextResult()**
This function returns the text result of the operation. For a GetNetText operation, this is the text of the HTTP item.

⚡ **NetMIME()**
This function returns the MIME type of the HTTP item.

⚡ **NetLastModDate()**
This function returns the last modified date string from the HTTP header for the item.

Note, however, that the NetTextResult, NetMIME, and NetLastModDate functions can be called only from the time NetDone or NetError report that the operation is complete until the next operation starts. Once the next operation starts, the results of the previous operation are discarded in order to preserve memory space.

One command can be used to abort a network operation that is in progress:

⚡ **NetAbort**
This command aborts a network operation without waiting for a result.

It is possible to have more than one operation active at a time. When two operations start, however, the Lingo script needs a way to identify them. After an operation starts and until the next operation begins, the following function can be called to retrieve a unique identifier for that operation:

⚡ **NetOperationID( )**
This function returns a unique identifier for the last asynchronous operation that was started.

Each of the functions NetDone, NetError, NetTextResult, NetMIME, NetLastModDate, and NetAbort take as an optional parameter the unique identifier of an operation unique identifier returned by NetOperationID.

In addition, there are two more asynchronous commands:

⚡ **GoToNetMovie** *uri*
This command retrieves and goes to a new Director movie from the network. The uri parameter is a uniform resource identifier that specifies the HTTP item that contains the movie. At present, only HTTP URLs are supported as valid uri parameters.

⚡ **GoToNetPage** *uri*
This command opens an arbitrary URI, whether it is a Director movie or not. Because this involves invoking the Internet browser to determine the type of item being opened and to handle it appropriately, it is a less efficient operation than GoToNetMovie, which assumes that the item must be a Director movie, and which therefore handles the entire operation within the Director Player.

APPENDIX C

Typical Download Times by Content and Channel Speed

The following tables provide details of typical download times for common modem throughputs, ISDN throughput for a Single B channel, and representative throughput on a shared 10.0 Mbps cable.

Table C.1	Common Modem Throughputs		
Channel Speed	Typical Content	Size	Download Time
14.4 Kbps	Small graphics and animation	30 KB	20 seconds
14.4 Kbps	Small complete title	100–200 KB	1–2 minutes
14.4 Kbps	Short video clip	500 KB	8–10 minutes
28.8 Kbps	Small graphics and animation	30 KB	10 seconds
28.8 Kbps	Small complete title	100–200 KB	30–60 seconds
28.8 Kbps	Short video clip	500 KB	2–3 minutes

Table C.2 ISDN Throughput When Using a Single B Channel			
Channel Speed	Typical Content	Size	Download Time
56 Kbps	Small graphics and animation	30 KB	5 seconds
56 Kbps	Small complete title	100–200 KB	15–30 seconds
56 Kbps	Short video clip	500 KB	1 minute
56 Kbps	Full-size title	1 MB	2 minutes

Table C.3 Representative Throughput on a Shared 10.0 Mbps Cable Modem or Ethernet LAN			
Channel Speed	Typical Content	Size	Download Time
1.5 Mbps	Small graphics and animation	30 KB	less than 1 second
1.5 Mbps	Small complete title	100–200 KB	1 second
1.5 Mbps	Short video clip	500 KB	3 seconds
1.5 Mbps	Full-size title	1 MB	6 seconds
1.5 Mbps	Title with full video and sound	2 MB	12 seconds
1.5 Mbps	MPEG video stream	—	Continuous

Note: 1.5 Mbps is also roughly the throughput of single-speed CD-ROM.

INDEX

Symbols

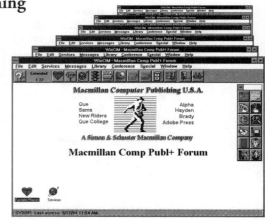

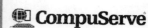

REGISTRATION CARD

Macromedia Shockwave for Director User's Guide

Name _____ Title _____

Company_____ Type of
business _____

Address _____

City/State/ZIP _____

E-mail/Internet _____ Phone_____

Would you like to be placed on our preferred mailing list? ❑ yes ❑ no

Have you used/purchased New Riders books before? ❑ yes ❑ no

Where did you purchase this book? Check one.
- ❑ Bookstore chain
- ❑ Wholesale club
- ❑ Independent bookstore
- ❑ College bookstore
- ❑ Computer store
- ❑ Other _____

What influenced your decision to purchase this title? _____
_____
_____

Which of the following operating systems do you use? Check all that apply.
- ❑ Windows 3.x
- ❑ Macintosh
- ❑ Windows 95
- ❑ SGI
- ❑ Windows NT
- ❑ Other _____

Please tell us the location of your shocked Web site(s). _____
_____
_____

Which of the following best describes your work environment? Check one.
- ❑ Self-employed
- ❑ Small business
- ❑ Large business

Which of the following do you create/develop for? Check all that apply.
- ❑ Games
- ❑ Print
- ❑ Motion pictures
- ❑ Other
- ❑ Web sites

What online services and Web sites do you visit on a regular basis? _____
_____

What trade shows do you attend? _____

What computer book titles do you consider your most valuable sources of information?
_____

What applications/technologies would you like to see us publish on in the future?
_____

Fax us at 1-317-581-4670

Check Us Out Online!

New Riders has emerged as a premier publisher of computer books for the professional computer user. Focusing on CAD/graphics/multimedia, communications/internetworking, and networking/operating systems, New Riders continues to provide expert advice on high-end topics and software.

Check out the online version of *New Riders' Official World Wide Yellow Pages, 1996 Edition* for the most engaging, entertaining, and informative sites on the Web! You can even add your own site!

Brave our site for the finest collection of CAD and 3D imagery produced today. Professionals from all over the world contribute to our gallery, which features new designs every month.

From Novell to Microsoft, New Riders publishes the training guides you need to attain your certification. Visit our site and try your hand at the CNE Endeavor, a test engine created by VFX Technologies, Inc. that enables you to measure what you know—and what you don't!

http://www.mcp.com/newriders

A Note from the Publisher and Authors

Macromedia's Shockwave for Director is bringing animation and true interactivity to the World Wide Web. We're pleased to bring you the *Macromedia Shockwave for Director User's Guide*, a step-by-step tutorial to help you shock your Web pages quickly!

The *Macromedia Shockwave for Director User's Guide* and its companion CD-ROM include everything you need to shock Director movies and embed them in Web pages. The Afterburner post-processor, which compresses Director movies and prepares them for uploading to an HTTP server, is included in both Macintosh and Windows formats on the CD-ROM.

To view shocked pages within your Web browser, you need the Shockwave plug-in. This plug-in is due to be released after the release date of the Netscape 2.0 Web browser, which had not occurred as this book went to press. A Macintosh version of the Shockwave plug-in was not yet available for inclusion with this book; however, the Windows and Windows 95 pre-release versions of the Shockwave plug-in is included on the CD-ROM.

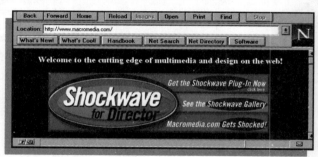

The Shockwave evolution has begun, and that is why we are bringing this title to you. To stay on top of this groundbreaking Web technology, please check out these two Web sites on a regular basis:

- ⚡ **Macromedia: http://www.macromedia.com.** By visiting the Macromedia site often, you'll be kept up-to-date with the most current Shockwave news and developments.

- ⚡ **New Riders Publishing: http://www.mcp.com/newriders**. This is where you'll find any updated information on the *Macromedia Shockwave for Director User's Guide*.

Thank you for selecting *Macromedia Shockwave for Director User's Guide*! Look for these upcoming Macromedia Director 5.0 books from New Riders:

- ⚡ *Inside Macromedia Director 5.0 with Lingo* (for Macintosh)

- ⚡ *Inside Macromedia Director 5.0 with Lingo* (for Windows)

- ⚡ *Lingo!* (An intermediate-to-advanced guide to using Lingo in Macromedia Director 5.0)